THE CADDOS
AND THEIR ANCESTORS

Artist's rendition of a scene of daily life in a Caddo village
(*Painting by Nola Davis, courtesy of the Texas Historical Commission*)

THE
Caddos
AND THEIR
Ancestors

ARCHAEOLOGY AND THE NATIVE PEOPLE
OF NORTHWEST LOUISIANA

JEFFREY S. GIRARD

Louisiana State University Press
Baton Rouge

Published with the assistance of the V. Ray Cardozier Fund

Published by Louisiana State University Press
Copyright © 2018 by Louisiana State University Press
All rights reserved
Manufactured in the United States of America
First printing

Designer: Laura Roubique Gleason
Typefaces: Minion Pro, text; Cervo Neue, display
Printer and binder: Sheridan Books

Unless otherwise noted, all photographs and line drawings are by the author.

Portions of chapter 2 first appeared in Jeffrey S. Girard et al., "Investigations at the Conly Site, a Middle Archaic Period Settlement in Northwest Louisiana," *Louisiana Archaeology* 32 (2011): 4–33, and are reprinted by permission of the editor. Portions of chapter 3 first appeared in Jeffrey S. Girard, "The Bellevue Site (16BO4): A Woodland Period Mound in Northwest Louisiana," *Louisiana Archaeology* 35 (2012): 53–78, and are reprinted by permission of the editor.

Library of Congress Cataloging-in-Publication Data are available from the Library of Congress.

ISBN 978-0-8071-6702-1 (cloth: alk. paper) — ISBN 978-0-8071-6703-8 (pdf) — ISBN 978-0-8071-6704-5 (epub)

The paper in this book meets the guidelines for permanence and durability of the Committee on Production Guidelines for Book Longevity of the Council on Library Resources. ∞

To Hiram F. "Pete" Gregory
and to the memory of Louis Baker

CONTENTS

PREFACE

In 1750, northwest Louisiana was populated primarily by American Indians, mostly native Caddo peoples, but with frequent visits by their western trading partners—particularly Wichitas and Comanches. Raids for slaves and booty were carried out by Osages from the north and Chickasaws from the east. Other eastern peoples (such as Pascagoulas, Apalachees, Coushattas, and Choctaws) began filtering into the region as they fled oppression from English colonists who were moving west of the Appalachian Mountains. European colonists and a relatively small number of African slaves were confined mostly to the small French colony and fort at Natchitoches and an even smaller Spanish presidio and mission thirty miles to the west.

The new settlers initially adapted to local conditions by attempting to understand the economic aspirations and social customs of the Caddos and learning from them new ways to interact with their physical environment. However, in the late eighteenth century, as American Indian populations declined and the number of peoples of European and African descent expanded, the cultural landscape of northwest Louisiana changed dramatically. By 1840, most of the Caddos and other American Indians had moved west, first into Texas, then Oklahoma (Indian Territory in the nineteenth century); and their cultures, dominant only a few generations earlier, now constituted a dimly remembered and highly romanticized past. French and Spanish colonial heritage had largely been supplanted by a now dominant Anglo-American culture as a result of the incorporation of Louisiana into the United States in 1803 and immigration of settlers from eastern portions of the upland South (Mississippi, Alabama, Tennessee, and Georgia).

The Industrial Revolution has been described as the most important event in human history. Not only did the early nineteenth century witness changes in how human beings provisioned themselves in material terms, but it also induced profound increases in the degree and intensity of interactions between different parts of the globe. The critical aspect of the Industrial Revolution for northwest Louisiana was the cotton industry. The Red River floodplain, formerly utilized for small-scale tobacco and indigo production as well as livestock grazing, became the setting of large-scale cotton plantations dependent on the labor of large numbers of African American slaves. Production of cotton fabrics was the first globally integrated manufacturing industry, and by the mid-nineteenth century northwest Louisiana was intertwined in a complex world economy. Acquisition and control of new lands became an economic necessity. The Caddos, their populations decimated by disease and impoverished from lacking sufficient means to cope with the developing economic and political order, were forced to the west, and the past centuries of their cultural heritage in Louisiana were preserved only in the objects and landscape alterations left behind in the archaeological record. The Caddo people persevered, however, and members of the present Caddo Nation of Oklahoma number more than five thousand.

In this book I trace the American Indian past of northwest Louisiana from the waning centuries of the Wisconsin ice age more than fourteen thousand years ago to the beginnings of the impact of the Industrial Age, about AD 1830. Framing a history in this manner is unusual, partly because of the vast scope of time encompassed. Histories of the region tend to commence with colonial times in the eighteenth century, or perhaps include a superficial description of American Indians with no consideration of time. This situation is due largely to the split between archaeology and history in regard to the study of the human past. Precolonial times are devoid of written records—the basic evidence of "history" in its narrow sense. The ancient past can only be known through interpretation of the material remains of human life—an endeavor undertaken by a different academic discipline and body of scholars. The result is a past dichotomized into "prehistory" and "history" with little consideration of how they interrelate. Archaeology is a profession with a limited number of practitioners, and few syntheses are available for general audiences to obtain a sense of the deep time and immense changes in human life that constitute prehistory. Although the appearance of French and Spanish colonists in the eighteenth century resulted in critical changes to traditional American Indian life in northwest Louisiana, in many respects the more profound break occurred about a century later with the beginnings of the modern industrial world, the time when the Caddos as a unified group were forced from the area, and it is at that point that I conclude this study.

With such a broad scope, it should be obvious that quite a few things are left out! My goal is to present a big picture of the changes in the major facets of human life and to limit my discussion to northwest Louisiana. Archaeologists have recognized a Caddo area that encompasses much of the southeastern wood-lands west of the Mississippi River valley in the present states of Arkansas, Louisiana, Texas, and Oklahoma. In Louisiana, Caddo culture extended from Texas east to the Ouachita River; and from Arkansas at least as far as the northern portions of Vernon and Rapides Parishes. Within this vast region, cultural continuity can be traced from the eighteenth century back at least one thousand years into the past. Peoples who resided within the Caddo area may not have been unified socially or politically, may not have shared the same way of life, and may not all have been direct ancestors of historically recognized Caddo groups. However, within this immense territory, human interactions were frequent and intensive, resulting in similarities in material culture patterns that have been identified in the archaeological record.

As I am trained primarily as an archaeologist, I attempt to tell this story by focusing on fascinating places at which archaeological investigations have been

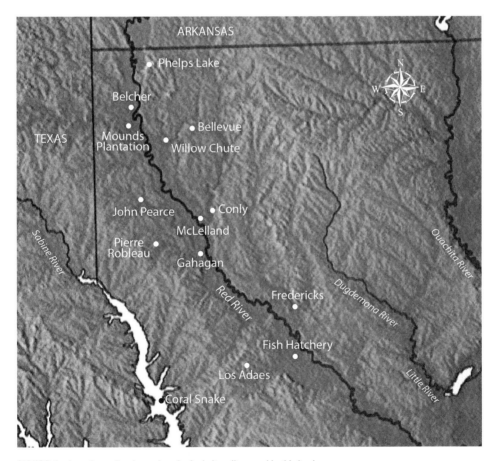

FIGURE 1. Locations of major archaeological sites discussed in this book

carried out (fig. 1). Since specific persons and events rarely are identifiable in the archaeological record, these take a minor role while I explore major changes regarding how human beings routinely lived their lives, exploited the environment, and interacted with their neighbors. Because many readers likely are not familiar with archaeological research, chapter 1 presents a brief look at the discipline of archaeology—its goals, and a few basics regarding how the archaeological record is "read," telling time when there are no documents, coins, or other objects upon which past people noted dates. Subsequent chapters treat major periods of time in chronological order. In each I discuss general aspects of the human condition for that time and include examples of investigated archaeological sites that have yielded especially important information.

Note: Terms italicized on first reference in the text can be found in the glossary.

ACKNOWLEDGMENTS

In 1989 the Louisiana Division of Archaeology, Department of Culture, Recreation, and Tourism established the Regional Archaeology Program. I served as regional archaeologist for the northwest part of the state for the next twenty-six years. This book is a product of the field work and syntheses of previous information carried out under the regional program. I am deeply grateful to the people of Louisiana and Northwestern State University for supporting us, and to my colleagues at the Division of Archaeology, with special thanks to Nancy Hawkins, who supervised and sustained the program over the years. Others who helped immensely include Joe Saunders, Duke Rivet, Kathleen Byrd, Tom Eubanks, Chip McGimsey, George Avery, Diana Greenlee, and Rob Mann.

Many people provided information about sites and artifacts, allowed access to their property, participated in projects, and provided other means of assistance. The two individuals to whom this book is dedicated need to be singled out: Dr. Hiram "Pete" Gregory has been a mentor, colleague, and friend throughout my time at Northwestern State University; and the late Louis Baker of Benton, Louisiana, was my partner in the field for many years. The Louisiana Archaeological Society has been critical in acquiring and public dissemination of much of the research reported in this book. I would especially like to thank Jameel Damlouji and David Jeane of the Northwest Chapter, John Guy Jr. of the West Chapter, and Nancy and Charles Affeltranger of the Central Chapter. I also want to thank editor Dennis Jones and the current LAS board of directors for permission to reproduce versions of two papers from the journal *Louisiana Archaeology* in chapters 2 and 3. Landowners and other people who have been of special help include Skipper Dickson, Mike Volentine, Bill Conly, and the Fredericks family. Nita Cole of the Louisiana State Exhibit Museum, Shreveport, and Pam Carter Carlisle of the Bossier Parish Library History Center provided access to collections and venues for public programs. Tim Perttula, Pete Gregory, and George Avery read drafts of the book text and made valuable suggestions. Finally, I would like to acknowledge the people of the present Caddo Nation, many of whom participate in the annual Caddo Conference and share knowledge of their history, traditions, and experiences.

THE CADDOS
AND THEIR ANCESTORS

1

ARCHAEOLOGY AND HUMAN HISTORY IN NORTHWEST LOUISIANA

When I first began research in Louisiana in the early 1990s, I made several presentations to school groups and sometimes asked the children if they knew the name of the American Indian people who inhabited northwest Louisiana (including Caddo Parish) prior to the nineteenth century. Sadly, relatively few could answer the question—familiar tribal names like Cherokees and Apaches came up most often. History classes made little reference to American Indians, and what was mentioned was of such a generic nature that little substantive knowledge was conveyed. Fortunately, school curricula have since changed, and today information on the American Indian past is routinely included.[1] Still, few people have much understanding of the early human past in Louisiana, a past that actually stretches back at least thirteen thousand years into the waning centuries of the Pleistocene geological era, when climate and landscape conditions differed markedly from modern times.

Written records only provide information regarding the last few centuries of at least twelve millennia of human existence in the Americas. For most of this long span of time, our knowledge comes exclusively through *archaeology*. For northwest Louisiana, we can trace strong continuities in artifact styles, patterns of settlement, and other cultural aspects of the Caddo people from the eighteenth century back at least to the tenth century. Prior to this, the archaeological record looks different, not necessarily because the Caddos were a new group of people who migrated in from elsewhere, but due to widespread changes that appear across much of the eastern portions of the continent at that time. After a brief glimpse offered by the somewhat enigmatic accounts of the sixteenth-century De Soto expedition, written references to the Caddos begin only in the late seventeenth century, and even then all writing was done by outsiders with limited understanding of Caddo culture. The ancient Caddos or their ancestors left no written record of themselves or their past.

Archaeologists investigate the human past through study of the material remains of human activity. Note that the focus is on the human past—archaeologists do not pursue, or study, the fossilized remains of dinosaurs or other animals and plants. Archaeology is most closely related to the disciplines of history and anthropology, whereas the study of fossil remains is in the domain of paleontology, a subject with direct connections to geology and biology. Methods and techniques from geology and biology are important in archaeological research, however, as are those from physics and other scientific as well as humanistic subjects.

A common misconception is that archaeology simply entails digging up old *artifacts.* Although archaeologists do study artifacts, of equal (or greater) importance are *features,* or the alterations to the landscape resulting from past human activities. These alterations include moving earth to form mounds and embankments; construction of houses and other structures; and digging pits for cooking, deposition of trash, or burial of the dead. It is the contexts of artifacts—their spatial relationships, environmental settings, and associations with archaeological features—that are crucial to the study of past human activities.

The basic data used in archaeological research are fragile and constantly being degraded and, in many instances, destroyed. Because data lie in the ground, modern alterations to the landscape significantly impact research. In fact, for archaeology, the process of doing research changes the record being studied. Places containing archaeological remains (*sites*) are essentially destroyed as they are excavated. What if reading a book caused the words to fall off the page and the book to crumble? In order to retain information, one would need to take very good notes. The same is true with archaeological research. It is not possible to put a site back after it has been excavated or artifacts removed from the surface. However, much can be learned if investigation takes place in a systematic and controlled manner, and all techniques and findings are recorded in notes, drawings, maps, and photographs (fig. 2). An undocumented collection of artifacts taken from the ground makes no more sense than a jumbled collection of words displaced from a book. The individual specimens, like individual words, constitute bits of information. But the story they tell relies on order and context.

Archaeological research differs from historical research in its emphasis on the study of material things rather than written documents. Most of the human past took place in times and places where no written records are available. These contexts, in which the archaeological record is the only record of what life was like, are commonly referred to as *prehistory.* There are no set boundaries to prehistory—written records extend back thousands of years in some areas such as the Middle East and Egypt. In northwest Louisiana, historic records begin with the

FIGURE 2. Students from Northwestern State University excavating and recording information at the Fish Hatchery 2 site in Natchitoches Parish

De Soto expedition in 1540–41, but are essentially absent again for more than 150 years until Spanish and French colonists began to arrive in the late seventeenth century. Archaeological research does not end when written records begin. It is becoming increasingly clear that studies of relatively recent periods of time have the potential to greatly expand our understanding of the past, particularly concerning issues and peoples often poorly represented in historical inquiries.

Although specific goals of archaeological research vary widely and rest upon a diverse array of theoretical premises and methods, most efforts are directed toward the following objectives:

1. *Reconstructing past activities.* At the most basic level is the attempt to understand archaeological data in terms of activities that constituted the daily lives of peoples in the past. Such activities include what kinds of foods were consumed and how they were prepared; what kinds of houses and other structures and facilities were built and used; and information about tools, containers, ornaments, clothing, and other items used by past peoples.

2. *Examining past social, economic, religious, and political organization.* On a slightly more abstract level are questions about past human relationships—how people were interconnected to meet environmental challenges and to interact with one another.

3. *Understanding past worldviews.* Of increasing concern in recent research are attempts to understand what people in the past thought about themselves, the natural world, and their place in the cosmos. How did these views relate to their organizations, technologies, and other aspects of life?

4. *Understanding and explaining change.* Understanding the dynamics of the past is a traditional concern of archaeological research. Archaeological data constitute a record of changes in worldviews, systems of organization, and human activities. A key aspect of research involves placing archaeological contexts in chronological order and constructing theories about how and why changes occurred.

Although the archaeological record is a contemporary phenomenon, it accrued over the course of several millennia, and it is important that we slice it into intervals of time that are small enough to be meaningful in terms of past human behavior. In some rare cases it is possible to isolate small-enough segments to interpret the record at a chronological resolution that we can almost relate to what was happening as if we had traveled back in time and were describing ongoing activities. The famous Pompeii site in Italy is probably the most extreme example—where the sudden burial of the city under volcanic lava and ash preserved buildings, objects, and even some of the people themselves. That situation is unique, however, and we almost always have to interpret sites that were abandoned, left to the elements to slowly decay, and, if we are fortunate, became buried by river deposits or sediments washing down from higher elevations. In much of the uplands of Louisiana, surfaces that existed several thousand years ago remain at or near the present surface. Not only does this situation result in the decay of most organic materials due to natural weathering processes, but exposure of surfaces results in the mixing together of materials from use of the landforms over long periods of time. It often is difficult, or impossible, to make sense of data in terms of short-term human behavior. Later in this book, I discuss the Conly site in Bienville Parish, where the remains of a large camp occupied approximately 7,500 years ago were buried relatively quickly by river alluvium, thus preserving normally perishable materials and precluding the possibility of later activities altering the record.

Even the Conly site, however, appears to have been used (perhaps intermittently) over the course of several centuries. The archaeological record is the fall-out of debris from intervals of human activity that vary in length. Redundancy in the kinds and spatial loci of activities results in distinctive patterns in the archaeological record. Different kinds of use of space produce different patterns. For example, a group of mobile hunter/gatherers may have inhabited the same ridge for a period of weeks or months on an annual basis, constructing hearths and temporary shelters. However, there might not have been anything on the ridge to constrain their use of space, and over the course of several yearly visits, remains of hearths and shelters would form archaeological features scattered randomly across the extent of the ridge. In contrast, a group of people living in the same space for longer periods might build more permanent structures and other facilities that organize their use of space. Certain activities, and discarding of debris, always took place in particular areas. Relative to the earlier scenario, a spatially organized archaeological record would result. It is for these reasons that archaeologists carefully record the spatial proveniences of everything that they find. Obviously in some cases, such as plowed fields, spatial relationships of artifacts are altered long after the materials are left behind by the people who used them. However, even in plowed fields, archaeological features often are found intact below the plowed sediments.

Anthropologist Eric Wolf wrote a book about European colonial expansion after the fifteenth century titled *Europe and the People without History.*[2] The concept of "people without history" is particularly apt because it is often inferred that portions of the earth other than Europe and connected parts of Asia and North Africa had relatively unchanging pasts in precolonial times. Cultural "others" have been objects of study in disciplines such as anthropology that focus on the conditions and ideas of contemporary peoples rather than on how those conditions and ideas developed through time. In schools and museums, American Indians are sometimes studied as part of "natural history" along with the landscape, plants, and fauna. The result is a static concept of the American Indian past in our popular imagination with little appreciation of the profound changes that took place over the centuries and how these changes were the products of both local events and more widespread regional interactions.

By the mid-twentieth century, archaeologists had developed ways to order the archaeological record into sequences—in other words, with enough research, it became possible to place things in relative chronological order. Determining sequences is partly based on a concept known as *stratigraphy,* or the simple idea that some landforms build up sediments through time, and thus the deeper we go below the ground surface, the older the materials. These situations generally are in river bottoms, where sediments suspended in water are deposited as flood-waters recede, constructing what are known as *natural levees.* Different flooding events sometimes leave sediments of varying color and texture that are readily identifiable. Long intervals between floods leave stable surfaces upon which vegetation grows and human groups place their camps or villages. Organic materials incorporated into such stable surfaces form dark-colored bands that we refer to as buried soils.

Unless there has been some sort of disturbance, the oldest occupations are found in the lowest strata that bear artifacts. Thus, in digging we encounter the past backward—the most recent occupations first, then we go back in time. However, determining how sequences related to calendar years was largely guesswork (some of which was found to be remarkably accurate!) until techniques such as *radiocarbon dating* and *dendrochronology* became refined in the later twentieth century, so that now we have much better interpretations of the age of archaeological sites.

Radiocarbon dating is of primary importance in northwest Louisiana. What is it, and what exactly does it date? The first thing to know is that, just as the name implies, the technique concerns carbon, the basic element of all life. Most carbon is carbon-12 (or C-12), a stable form found in all living things. Cosmic rays from the sun, however, produce an unstable "radioactive" form of carbon called carbon-14 (or C-14). Plants absorb C-14 through photosynthesis; animals obtain it by eating plants. The ratio of C-14 to C-12 atoms is very small, but it is the same in all living things. C-14 is unstable and diminishes at a known rate—approximately half decays over a span of 5,730 years (the "half-life"). Solar radiation keeps the C-14/C-12 ratio in the atmosphere constant (with minor, but important, exceptions noted below). However, once a living organism dies, it no longer receives C-14 from the atmosphere, and thus the C-14/C-12 ratio diminishes. Since this decay occurs at a known rate, measurement of the C-14/C-12 ratio in charcoal or other organic material provides a measure of the elapsed time since the organism died. After about ten half-lives (in the range of 60,000 to 80,000 years), C-14 amounts are too small to be counted reliably, and thus other dating techniques must be used. Fortunately, this remote time is long prior to the earliest evidence of any human presence in North America.

Counting C-14 atoms is carried out in a radiocarbon laboratory. The most efficient way that this is done today is by a technique known as Accelerated Mass Spectrometry, or AMS. The procedure is subject to statistical uncertainty, and results are reported as an interval rather than an exact age in years—for example, "700 ± 30 years BP (before present)" means that there is a 66.7 percent chance that the true date lies somewhere between 670 and 730 years ago (one standard deviation); and there is a 95 percent chance that it lies between 640 and 760 years ago (two standard deviations). A complicating factor, however, is that we now know that the percentage of C-14 in the atmosphere has varied a little over time, and thus radiocarbon years are not exactly the same as calendar years. The discrepancy is greater the further we go back in time. On the positive side, we also know the degree of this variation by taking radiocarbon samples from wood that has been dated through dendrochronology. Calibration curves have been produced whereby we can translate radiocarbon years into calendar years. For example, using the CALIB method of calibration (there are others, but results are similar), a radiocarbon age of 700 ± 30 BP likely would fall somewhere in the AD 1271–1297 interval.

Note that what generally is dated is charcoal, or perhaps bone or shell—it must be something organic. We cannot get radiocarbon dates from stone or

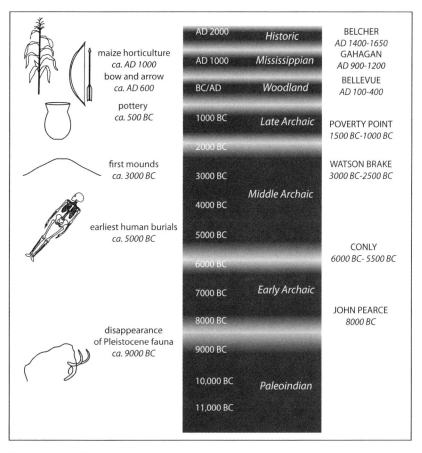

FIGURE 3. Timeline of general cultural periods in Louisiana

pottery (unless organic material has been preserved on them). In order to date nonorganic artifacts, we must establish an association between the datable material and other things. In other words, we must infer that they were left behind at the same general time. If objects are removed from an archaeological site without proper recording of their contexts and associations, they cannot be reliably dated.

From our present perspective, we can look back and organize the human past into a sequence of periods within which we are able to make generalizations about the ways people interacted with other people and the landscape. In Louisiana and the southeastern United States in general, we commonly recognize five major divisions: the Paleoindian period (ca. 11,500–8000 BC), the Archaic period (ca. 8000–500 BC), the Woodland period (ca. 500 BC–AD 900), the Mississippian period (ca. AD 900–1650), and the Historic period (ca. AD 1650 to present) (fig. 3). These periods can be subdivided in various ways depending on the amount and nature of evidence for different regions. The earliest periods are of great length and encompass intervals when changes appear to have taken place very slowly, social interactions were few and sporadic, and similar lifeways prevailed across vast areas. Through time we see greater diversity, a faster tempo of change, and more connections between groups. Although our notion of these trends may partly reflect the greater amount of information available for more recent times, an overall rise in population through time along with escalating numbers and frequencies of linkages and interdependencies between people across the landscape undoubtedly took place.

2

THE EARLIEST PEOPLES OF NORTHWEST LOUISIANA (CA. 11,500–500 BC)

When did the first people arrive in Louisiana, and where did they originate? These are difficult questions, and the answers continue to be vigorously debated. Research on the earliest period of human settlement presents many challenges, in part, due to the nature of the environment.[1] Although many areas of the state are dominated by upland landforms of sufficient age to contain evidence of these early peoples, most sites in upland settings are located on stable or eroding surfaces where artifacts from later occupations have become mixed with those of earlier times. Exposure of the surfaces for millennia greatly limits or precludes preservation of features with charcoal or other organic materials. The opposite problem relates to the major river floodplains. Massive sediment deposition and reworking of deposits by channel changes either destroy evidence of the earliest human occupations or bury it too deeply to be discovered by current investigative techniques. Special challenges exist along the Gulf coast. Due to sea-level rises and land subsidence, coastal landforms that existed during the late Pleistocene now lie beneath many feet of water. There are hints that some very early sites exist in coastal waters, but we have not yet conducted sufficient research to understand how these areas were used by early human groups.

Paleoindian Life at the End of the Ice Ages

Although a few archaeological sites in both North and South America date prior to 11,500 BC, it is not possible to identify stone tools or other material traits that are distinctively associated with these earliest human occupations. Archaeologists have not found evidence for human activity of that antiquity in northwest Louisiana, despite the existence of *Pleistocene* and *Tertiary* upland landforms of sufficient age to contain such remains. However, there is ample evidence in the form of stone tools that the area was visited during the time period that we refer to as the Paleoindian period, which dates roughly between 11,500 and 8000 BC.

The distinctive Clovis *points* and associated tool forms (*scrapers, gravers,* and *knives*), once considered to represent the first evidence of human occupation in North America, were made and used during the period from approximately 11,500 to 10,900 BC. The Clovis point, named after a site near the town of Clovis in eastern New Mexico where it was first found, is distinguished by its distinctive outline and "fluted" flake scar originating at the base. Local artifact collectors have found several specimens, but, with one exception, none have been recovered in areas not mixed with later materials. The best recorded context is from the John Pearce site located near Cypress Bayou in southern Caddo Parish, where Clarence Webb[2] and colleagues conducted excavations in the 1960s. They found two possible Clovis points at the base of what appeared to be a pit that had been made by the Paleoindian inhabitants. It should be noted, however, that they also found two points of a later type known as San Patrice in the upper portions of the pit, and they did not encounter charcoal for possible radiocarbon dating.

While conducting research on Peason Ridge in southern Sabine Parish during the 1980s, archaeologists found another possible small Clovis-period camp at the Eagle Hill II site. They recovered one complete Clovis point and two base fragments along with scrapers and chert flakes used as cutting tools. Unfortunately, due to the eroded condition of the site, archaeological features and other evidence of occupation were not present.

A wider range of tool forms relates to the period from the latter part of the Paleoindian period (ca. 10,900–8000 BC). Several point forms, some fluted and others not, are thought to relate to this time. Most common are San Patrice points, which appeared across most of Louisiana and surrounding areas by about 8000 BC (fig. 4). It is not known how long these tools continued to be manufactured and used, but, given the large number found, they likely lasted for several centuries. Unlike Clovis points, San Patrice points generally are made from local chert stream *pebbles,* and thus are small in size relative to the earlier forms. Beveling and variation in shapes of the margins suggest that they were routinely resharpened, and thus probably served as cutting tools in addition to weaponry. San Patrice points were named by Clarence Webb from specimens found along Bayou San Patrice in DeSoto Parish. Excavations by Webb and colleagues at the John Pearce site provided a look at a small camp occupied during this period. In addition to the Clovis points noted earlier, the excavators also recovered approximately forty San Patrice points along with a variety of scraping tools, gravers, flake knives, and *perforators.* They identified two archaeological features that probably were pits dug by the site inhabitants but found no evidence of structures or hearths, suggesting that the site was an intermittently occupied camp.

FIGURE 4. Possible Clovis (*top left*) and San Patrice points from the John Pearce site, Caddo Parish (*Items in Wayne Roberts Collection, Louisiana State Exhibit Museum, Shreveport*)

The Paleoindian period dates to the end of the Pleistocene geological era, a time characterized by considerable environmental change. By about 12,000 BC, Ice Age climatic conditions effectively ended, and boreal forests (dominated by spruce and fir) gradually changed to modern mixed-forest uplands and cypress-gum forest bottomlands. The possible role of now-extinct Pleistocene animals in the Paleoindian diet has been the subject of considerable research and discussion. Paleoindians were once thought to have been primarily "big-game" hunters who targeted large animals such as mastodons and mammoths. Although there is clear evidence that large-game hunting did occur in some portions of North America, it now seems likely that Paleoindians in the Southeast exploited a broader range of food resources. Unfortunately, we have no direct information from Louisiana regarding the kinds of foods eaten during this period.

The apparent lack of accumulation of significant material at any particular place in the landscape has been interpreted as reflecting high residential mobility of the Paleoindian groups as they exploited extensive and dispersed food resources. It must be admitted, however, that we know very little about human life for this time due to the paucity of investigations. The discovery and systematic study of a few key sites could dramatically enhance our knowledge of the first people of the region. Understanding the most ancient times of the human past awaits archaeologists of the future.

Early Hunting, Fishing, and Gathering: The Archaic Period

The very long interval from about 8000 to 500 BC is referred to as the Archaic period. In many ways this is a continuation of Paleoindian times as people made their livings by hunting, fishing, and gathering wild plant foods. Little or no domestication of plants took place, and people did not make ceramic containers. However, they adopted a wider range of stone tool forms, including ground and polished items such as *axes, grinding stones,* and *celts.* The earliest-known ornamental and ritual items date from this period, particularly polished stone beads, some in the shape of animals. For many years, research on the Archaic period was rather mundane, consisting largely of attempts to place projectile points and other stone tools in correct chronological order. Although this remains a research goal of primary importance, recent work has provided some of the most detailed and interesting information about human life for any period of Louisiana prehistory.

As noted earlier, Paleoindian groups are thought to have been small and highly mobile, which partially accounts for why we find only limited numbers of their artifacts scattered widely across the landscape. Many possessions are a burden for peoples who change their residences frequently in order to exploit resources in different regions. There is evidence, however, that as time passed during the Archaic period, people in Louisiana moved less frequently and perhaps remained in well-defined territories. Rather than ranging widely, they began to focus on areas where multiple resources were found together. From relatively permanent base camps they could send out task groups to acquire and bring back food and other necessary materials that were located at greater distances. Such a change in lifeways produced a different archaeological record—one containing greater amounts of material at specific locations. As people inhabited places repeatedly or for longer intervals, they increasingly constructed facilities and utilized restricted areas within camps for distinct purposes such as cooking, tool-making, shelter, trash deposition, and burial of the dead. Resulting archaeological sites are thus better organized spatially and contain features in addition to accumulations of artifacts.

Utilizing analogies with modern peoples whose economies are based primarily on hunting and gathering, it seems likely that Archaic-period peoples were organized into family groups that were more complex and inclusive than the *nuclear families* of individual households that are most common today. Much anthropological research has gone into understanding kinship because of its importance in almost all societies. Study and classification of different kinship systems illuminate how relationships and notions of genealogical descent are recognized and emphasized by different peoples. In modern Western societies we generally have *bilateral descent* systems, meaning that families of both our mothers and fathers are considered related, although traditionally there has been a *patrilineal* emphasis, with more importance (including passing on of names) placed on descent through the male line. In contrast, the eighteenth-century Hasinai Caddos of the Neches-Angelina region in East Texas emphasized *matrilineal* descent, but the system is not well understood and apparently differed between Caddo groups.[3]

During the Archaic period, it is likely that some groups formed larger communities consisting of multiple descent groups. These communities, in turn, developed into tribes that, although lacking formal political systems, had some form of pantribal traditions or institutions. Activities such as marriages, military engagements, trade and exchange, and ritual may have been coordinated at the tribal level. However, social boundaries and group affiliation probably were flexible, and connections of varying strength existed at differing spatial scales and persisted for varying lengths of time. Because of the fluid nature of group affiliation and the mobility of populations, it generally is not possible to recognize and delimit past "territories" for the Archaic period. We are able to identify sites throughout upland landforms in northwest Louisiana but cannot isolate distinct social or political groups. However, by asking questions about the material consequences of different kinds of organizations, archaeologists infer how past societies were organized. What was the nature of leadership positions? Who made decisions about critical resources (particularly food)? Who had control of ritual and knowledge, enforced justice, or had the authority to formally communicate with outsiders? How were military actions coordinated and territorial boundaries established? Is there evidence of wealth accumulation by particular groups or individuals? Do we recover objects that appear to be of special ritual or symbolic importance? If so, do these appear in burials, perhaps of only limited numbers of individuals? Are objects made from nonlocal raw materials present at some sites, or at all sites? The nature and extent of political control by certain groups and individuals likely differed between communities and transformed through time during the Archaic period, and we are just beginning to gain insights about these changes.

By what we call the "Middle" Archaic period, or the time between approximately 6000 and 2000 BC, American Indians in some portions of northwest Louisiana began to live for sustained periods in areas where multiple food resources were available. As people made more intensive use of particular places in the landscape, they left behind archaeological sites that contain abundant and diverse tool and faunal assemblages and numerous archaeological features, including human burials. One of the most remarkable of these places in northwest Louisiana—indeed, one of the most noteworthy in the southeastern United States—is the Conly site.

The Conly Site: An Archaic-Period Residential Camp and Cemetery

As noted for Paleoindian times, Archaic-period sites in Louisiana tend to be situated in upland settings that have undergone little or no sedimentation during the *Holocene*.[4] Consequently, there is often a jumble of materials from long time spans, making it difficult to understand regional chronologies or changes in human lifeways. The Conly site is an exception. The site sits in the southwestern corner of Bienville Parish on the edge of Loggy Bayou, the name of the lower portion of a major tributary of Red River known as Bayou Dorcheat (fig. 5). Between approximately 6200 and 5400 BC, the inhabitants resided on a surface now buried beneath 3–4 m (10–13 ft) of alluvial sediments. Over the course of several hundred years, fire-cracked rock, animal bone, and clusters of mussel shell accumulated in a 30–50 cm (12–20 in)–thick layer that is now exposed in the riverbank for a distance of approximately 100 m (328 ft). People also left stone tools and *chipping debris,* but in surprisingly small numbers given the size of the site and density of food remains. Several human burials, the earliest known in Louisiana, have been found at this unique location.

The deeply buried dark-colored stratum of earth exposed in the bank is a dark-gray silty clay loam that represents a buried soil horizon that developed on a landform of Tertiary or Pleistocene age. At the time the site was occupied, the landform was a gently sloping rise in the Loggy Bayou floodplain. Soils develop when a surface remains stable or builds up very slowly for a sufficiently long period of time for vegetation to grow, die, and decay in the sediments. A dark (organically rich) layer forms, and debris from human activities also may be incorporated into this upper soil horizon. Soil horizons that contain concentrations of artifacts and organic materials are often referred to as *middens* by archaeologists. If local conditions change and the landform becomes subject to rapid flooding, floodwaters may deposit one or more layers of sediment over the top of the dark

FIGURE 5. Three-dimensional model of the setting of the Conly site using LIDAR elevation data

layer. This is what happened at the Conly site, eventually leaving the midden buried beneath 3.6–4.6 m (12–15 ft) of reddish-brown alluvial (stream-deposited) clay. This clay has the distinctive reddish-brown color of Red River sediments, indicating that it resulted from floodwaters backing up from the Red River. Extensive leaching (displacement) of carbonates from the clay, the absence of artifacts postdating the Middle Archaic period, and the excellent preservation of faunal remains (animal bone and antler) suggest that burial of the site began during the Middle Holocene rather than many years after the area was abandoned. In fact, it is possible that the site's increasing propensity for flooding might be the reason the inhabitants decided to settle elsewhere.

The landowner, Bill Conly, brought the site to the attention of archaeologists in the late 1970s, and Clarence Webb of Shreveport funded a limited investigation in 1980. Archaeologists excavated two test units and three features exposed in the bank of Loggy Bayou. Unfortunately, no one analyzed the recovered materials, and only an unpublished summary of the fieldwork was produced following the work.

I first saw the site in 1994, when other archaeologists working in the area noted that bone and artifacts were eroding from the bank. At the time, Loggy Bayou was approximately 3–4 m (10–13 ft) below the base of the dark midden layer, which was exposed in the nearly vertical bank. Slow erosion through slumping was ongoing, and there was evidence that treasure hunters were digging holes to look for projectile points. Given the immense logistical difficulties for investigations, it did not appear feasible to carry out excavations at that time, and the bank slumped slowly for the next five years.

In the summer of 1999, Skipper Dickson, a local landowner with a keen interest in the history and landscape of the region, notified me that water levels of Loggy Bayou had risen following closure of Lock and Dam No. 4 on the Red River. The site now was rapidly eroding, and treasure hunters had easy access to its contents. Dickson identified remnants of two human burials exposed in the bank. After consultation with the Caddo Nation of Oklahoma, we excavated the remaining exposed bone (only portions of the legs) from one of the burials (Burial 1 in fig. 6). Because it was clear that the Conly site contained an immense amount of important data that needed to be extracted in a controlled and careful manner, we directed our efforts toward preserving the site rather than hastily excavating the remaining deposits.

Human bone, part of the cranium apparently from a small child, was also found a short distance upstream where a point of land projected into the bayou. The clay overburden had eroded from this point, leaving the midden exposed on the surface. We decided to conduct additional investigations on this surface for several reasons. First, the work would provide better data on the nature of the deposits and the ongoing impacts to the site. Second, we were likely to recover charcoal or other organic material in a context that would allow us to obtain radiocarbon dates. Third, we could explore the area where the cranium was found to see if more of the burial remained. And finally, there was the possibility that additional features and artifacts were present that were not visible at the surface. The project also would enable us to acquire the data necessary to nominate the site to the National Register of Historic Places. In the fall of 1999, I headed the work as part of the Regional Archaeology Program based at Northwestern State University of Louisiana. The Louisiana Division of Archaeology and the National Park Service provided funding. In the field, an experienced colleague, Louis Baker of Benton, Louisiana, and several other members of the Louisiana and Texas archaeological societies assisted with the excavations. The first task was

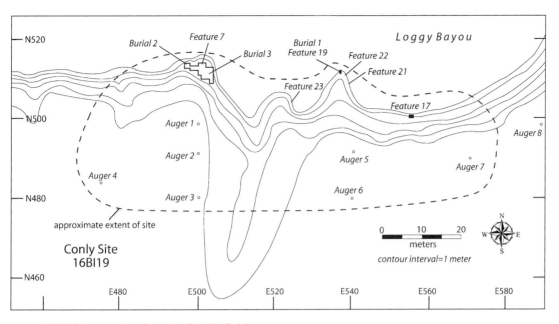

FIGURE 6. Map of the Conly site, Bienville Parish

carried out by Thurman Allen and Mark Bordelon, soil scientists with the Natural Resources Conservation Service, U.S. Department of Agriculture, who excavated a series of auger tests through the clay to determine how much of the site remained beneath the existing bluff. They were able to identify the top of the buried landform in all of the augers (see fig. 6). Dark midden deposits were present to about 25 m (82 ft) from the bluff but were not detected farther back.

The block excavation consisted of fourteen 1 × 1 m squares in the exposed midden—a very dark gray clay loam containing abundant fire-cracked rock, charred plant remains, animal bone, and a few chipped stone artifacts (fig. 7). Excavation to the base of the midden revealed four large zones, or features, where dark sediments extended significantly deeper than in surrounding areas. We found several smaller circular dark features as well. The larger features obviously were pits that had been excavated into the site surface by the Archaic-period people. One, Feature 7, was approximately 1.9 m (a little over 6 ft) in diameter and 1.2 m (4 ft) deep and contained much of the same kinds of material as the midden, but in higher densities. We discovered clusters of freshwater mussel shell and numerous deer antlers that had been dumped or placed at the base of the pit. Radiocarbon analysis on charcoal from the pit dated to 6205–5076 BC.

Another pit feature, approximately the same size, was actively eroding from the stream bank and had to be excavated from a boat. Others were only partially

FIGURE 7. Archaeologists Louis Baker and David Jeane excavating the Conly site on the bank of Loggy Bayou

exposed by the excavations and were not explored further. The original functions of the large pit features are not clear. We encountered ash lenses in two of the pits and found that greater percentages of bone were charred in the pits than in the midden. However, the pit margins were not hardened and discolored, and we do not believe that burning took place within these features. The Conly site inhabitants eventually filled the pits with trash, mostly food remains. They dumped more fish and turtle bone in the pits relative to the general midden scatter, where deer bone was dominant. Why this is the case is not clear—perhaps the fish remains smelled bad, and the inhabitants were reluctant to pollute the bayou adjacent to the site.

We were successful in locating the remainder of the burial pertaining to the cranium of the child found earlier on the bank (Burial 2). Most of the rest of the bone remained articulated, but several ribs had been displaced, and the lower leg and feet bones were in a jumble. It appeared that the burial had been disturbed by a burrowing animal. The remains were those of a small child who had been buried with the head oriented slightly northwest of current magnetic north. The arms were bent at the elbows with the hands placed over the pelvis. The bones were sent to Texas A&M University and studied by physical anthropologists Michelle Raisor and C. Gentry Steele. On the basis of size measurements and degree of ossification, they estimated that the child was about five years old. Scattered charcoal recovered from the area around the burial was submitted for radiocarbon analysis and yielded a date of 6363–5722 BC. However, the charcoal might have filtered down from the overlying midden, or the burial might have been covered with sediment containing the charcoal—thus, it does not necessarily relate to the burial event.

On the south side of Feature 7 we encountered another human burial, this one of a young female, probably in her late teens or early twenties when she died (Burial 3 in fig. 6; fig. 8). She had been placed in the same manner as the child—oriented approximately on a north-south axis, but unlike the child, her head was to the south with her face turned to the west. Although many of the bones had

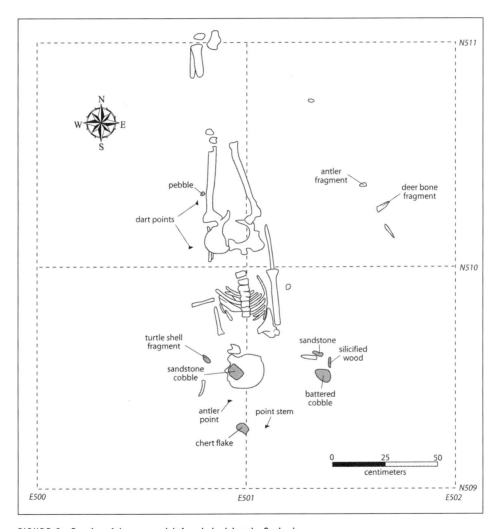

FIGURE 8. Drawing of the young adult female burial at the Conly site

been displaced, it appeared that the arms were positioned parallel to the upper body with the hands beneath the pelvis. Animal burrowing was evident in the left shoulder area, where the humerus, scapula, clavicle, and several ribs were either missing or out of place. Only a fragment of a mandible was present, also likely a result of this burrowing. Other damage was evident in the lower portion of the body as most bones associated with the lower legs and feet were displaced or missing. The burial lay within the dark midden sediments, and no evidence of a burial pit could be discerned. Several animal bone fragments and artifacts were found near the skeletal remains, but we could not determine which, if any, might have been deliberate inclusions as burial offerings. Artifacts consisted of a chert flake and projectile-point stem found south of the cranium; a polished antler tip, also found south of the cranium; and a battered quartz *cobble* found east of the cranium. We found two dart points in the midden above the burial adjacent to the pelvis and upper left femur. A sample of scattered charcoal recovered in the deposits surrounding the burial dated between 5640 and 5555 BC. As with Burial 2, the charcoal does not necessarily relate to the burial event but may have been introduced with the sediments used to cover the burial, or may have filtered down later from the overlying midden.

The human remains from the Conly site are the earliest yet identified in Louisiana, and among the earliest from the southeastern United States. The small sample and fragmented nature of most of the remains limit interpretations about the represented populations. Raisor and Steele noted that the individual represented in Burial 3 was short by today's standards but comparable to the mean stature of other hunter/gatherer populations. They also noted that the relatively long and narrow braincase of this individual closely resembles the braincase shape of other Early Archaic and Paleoindian remains. Following analysis, the skeletal remains were reburied near the site by members of the modern Caddo Nation.

Animal bones recovered from the Conly site were numerous and in an excellent state of preservation. Susan Scott and Ed Jackson from the University of Southern Mississippi analyzed a large sample of the bones. Not surprisingly, fish and deer dominate the assemblage. Freshwater drum was a favorite of the site inhabitants, but also important were slackwater species such as bullhead catfish, gar, bowfin, and buffalo fish. Turtle remains from a variety of species, as well as crawfish, were also present. Analysis of the ages of represented deer led Scott and Jackson to conclude that the Conly site was inhabited during all seasons. This conclusion was corroborated by Gary L. Stringer of the University of Louisiana at Monroe, who examined fish otoliths preserved at the site. *Otoliths* are made of calcium carbonate and were particularly well represented at the Conly site. Freshwater drum and other fish could have been obtained from the main channel of Loggy Bayou by use of a hook and line, spearing, use of weirs, traps, or nets, or some combination of these techniques. The presence of very small fish in the discarded remains, fish that likely were too small to be of significant use as food, suggests use of nets and discarding of small specimens in the large pits. The inhabitants might have obtained other species from an old channel scar that is present between Loggy Bayou and the uplands. Judging by the magnitude of the arc, the scar probably relates to a stream of Pleistocene age. If so, it likely was a backwater slough at the time the site was occupied, perhaps a key source area for the aquatic fauna that constituted a large portion of the inhabitants' diet. Spearing may have been one of the techniques employed in this setting.

Samples of charred plant material recovered from *flotation processing* and screening were analyzed by Phil Dering of Texas A&M. Charred hickory nutshell was by far the most abundant material represented. Acorn shell, hackberry nutlets, and wood fragments were present in small quantities (wood included white oak, hackberry, hickory, and elm). Despite the excellent preservation, Dering's team identified none of the oily and starchy seed plants often found in later times in the Southeast. Hickory nuts can be used for both their oil and nut meat. Because of the difficulties with storing and transporting nut oil, it has been argued that mobile Archaic-period groups probably processed most nuts for meat. Historic American Indians in the Southeast often pounded nuts into powder and mixed it with other foods for consumption. The high amount of charring of the nutshell refuse might have resulted from parching nuts on hot rocks. Parching involves heating nuts to a point where fungi, larvae, and other agents of deterioration are destroyed, enabling storage for longer periods. Ideally, nuts should be removed before shells are charred, but accidental charring may have occurred frequently. Dering also noted that discarded nutshells might have been used as fuel for hearths. We found angular chunks of fire-cracked sandstone that could have resulted from parching or cooking throughout the midden and large pit features.

In contrast to the abundance of food remains, the excavations yielded relatively few stone artifacts at the Conly site (fig. 9). The recovered stemmed dart points can be assigned to several types. Possible forms include Macon, Bulverde, Carrollton, Jones Creek, and Ellis. All of these were made from local chert pebbles. A couple of fragmented specimens made from a nonlocal stone, novaculite from the Ouachita Mountains, have stems with concave bases suggestive of Johnson points, a type more common in southern Arkansas and eastern Oklahoma.

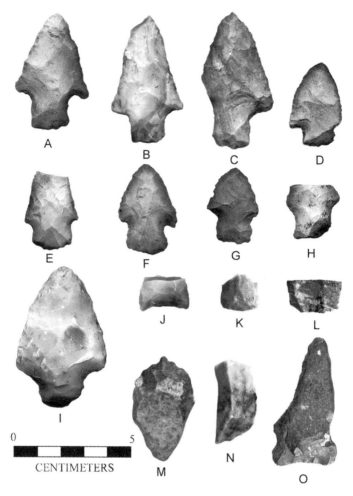

FIGURE 9. Chipped stone tools from the Conly site: dart points (A–I); dart-point stem fragments (J–L); graver (M); scrapers (N–O)

Notably absent are the distinctive blade-notched Evans points found at the earliest mound sites in Louisiana, which date a few millennia later than the Conly site. Other recovered stone tools include a small number of pebble scrapers, cobble grinding stones, pitted cobbles, hammerstones, and a full-grooved axe (fig. 10). The scraping tools may have been used for processing animal hides; the grinding stones for pulverizing nuts; and the axe for felling small trees and other woodworking tasks.

Normally ubiquitous at Archaic-period sites are the by-products of stone-tool manufacture—flakes, *spalls,* and thick-flaked pebbles discarded before being finished into functional tools (*blanks* or *preforms*). Such debris was very sparse at

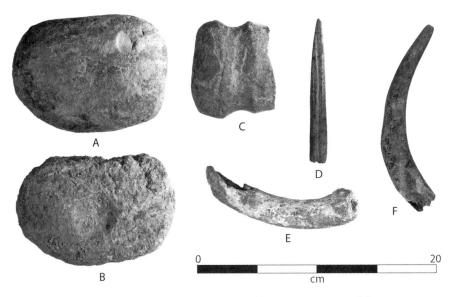

FIGURE 10. Artifacts from the Conly site: grinding stone (A); pitted grinding stone (B); grooved axe fragment (C); bone awl (D); antler handle (E); antler flaking tool (F)

the Conly site and consisted primarily of small chert flakes, most of which appear to have resulted from resharpening tools rather than making them directly from local pebbles or cobbles. The absence of specimens broken and discarded during production further indicates that the inhabitants carried out most activities relating to stone tool manufacture elsewhere.

One of the more interesting aspects of the Conly site is the excellent preservation of tools, and possibly ornaments, made from bone and antler—materials that often do not survive in the acidic upland soils of northwest Louisiana. Modified bone and antler artifacts were analyzed by Nathanael Heller of R. Christopher Goodwin and Associates. Heller identified handles made from deer antler, antler flakers, bone points and awls, and two possibly decorated objects of unknown function. He also noted that a few pointed tools were made from fish spines.

Pits full of food remains, human burials, tools of stone, bone, and antler all found together distinguish the Conly site from anything we see earlier in the archaeological record of northwest Louisiana. The evidence indicates that beginning about 6000 BC some places in the landscape began to be used far more intensively than others. But what do we mean by "intensively"? Well, it does not necessarily imply that one group of people lived continuously at the site during all seasons for decades or centuries. The food remains indicate that people lived or visited there during all seasons but not necessarily on a continuous basis. It is possible that groups still changed residences seasonally. However, for some periods within the total span of occupation, the site was used during colder months, at other periods during warmer months. It also is possible that a single group resided at the Conly site continually for several years (perhaps until local resources were depleted), moved elsewhere, and then reoccupied the site several years later, when resources such as fish and mammal populations, and perhaps timber, had rejuvenated enough to make it worthwhile again. Judging the tempo of use of particular places in the landscape is tricky. Future work may result in the discovery of contemporary sites in the region, thereby enabling a better picture of the overall pattern of settlement.

Although we do not know the details, it is evident that, early in the Middle Archaic period, human populations in northwestern Louisiana began to concentrate in areas where multiple food resources were available. A settlement system developed where movement of resources to habitation areas became more important than movement of habitation areas between resource areas. Why the change? Several hypotheses can be offered.

Increasingly warm and dry conditions, well demonstrated in the southern Plains to the west at this time, may have had some effect on northwest Louisiana. If upland food resources were becoming patchier and less reliable, some groups may have found it advantageous to utilize intensively those areas where multiple resources were known to be abundant. Researchers have noted a shift from Early Archaic–period exploitation of small terrestrial mammals to a broadened subsistence base during the Middle Archaic, consisting of procurement of both deer and riverine resources concentrated in floodplain environments.[5] The Conly site offered easy access to major floodplain, backwater slough, and upland microenvironments. Unfortunately for this suggestion, however, we have no direct evidence that Middle Holocene climatic conditions in Louisiana differed significantly from those today. The Conly site inhabitants exploited a wide range of fauna, but all of the species are still present in the modern landscape. Recent studies suggest that climatic changes in the Middle Holocene had variable effects on the landscape.[6] Another possibility is that harsher conditions in the southern Plains resulted in an influx of people into the adjacent woodlands, where conditions remained more amenable to settlement. Because this would have resulted in greater regional population levels, people might have become increasingly territorial, restricting the ranges within which they could exploit resources and forcing them to focus on the most favorable places. It also has been argued that Middle Holocene climatic conditions in the southeastern United States caused increased meandering of river channels and the emergence of *backswamp* and *oxbow environments* rich in biotic resources that became focal points for human exploitation.[7] The Conly site represents changing human patterns of settlement and resource use in northwest Louisiana; we have a long way to go before we understand why the change occurred.

It is important to note the degree to which our interpretation of the Conly site hinges on its unique (at least at this time) depositional context and consequent degree of preservation. The relatively rapid burial of the site not only precluded the incorporation of later materials but also preserved bone and shell, which normally deteriorate in northwest Louisiana's acidic upland soils. The same range of activities that resulted in the Conly site would have left a very different archaeological record in a nondepositional environment. Lacking bone (and likely evidence of the shallow burials), the site would have contained only a small number of stone tools and chipping debris, and we probably would have only interpreted it as a briefly occupied camp. There is also the possibility that the site would have been repeatedly utilized over the succeeding millennia and the Middle Archaic–period occupation was completely masked by more abundant later materials.

Places relating exclusively to the Middle Archaic period that contain numerous intact features, abundant and well-preserved faunal and botanical remains, and ample charcoal for dating are extremely rare in the southeastern United States. Research has demonstrated that the Conly site has all of these attributes. Human remains present at the site are the earliest yet found in Louisiana and among the most ancient in the eastern United States. These characteristics not only impart high scientific value to the site but also make it of great importance to the cultural heritage of the modern Caddo Nation and other American Indian groups who lived in the region. After the fieldwork was completed, landowner Bill Conly donated an archaeological conservation servitude to the Louisiana Archaeological Conservancy. This donation enabled a project jointly funded by the U.S. Army Corps of Engineers and the State of Louisiana to construct a rock retaining dam to prevent slumping of the Loggy Bayou bank where the remainder of the site is exposed. This dam was constructed in the summer of 2003, and the site has been saved for the future.

3

THE WOODLAND PERIOD AND EARLY MOUNDS IN NORTHWEST LOUISIANA (CA. 500 BC–AD 900)

Since at least the late eighteenth century, people have been fascinated by the earthen *mounds* constructed throughout the Southeast and Midwest. Many mounds are large and complex, and their construction obviously entailed considerable engineering skill and labor. Such endeavors were once thought to be beyond the capabilities of American Indians, and it was postulated that a sophisticated mound-builder culture formerly existed but was decimated by more primitive Indians prior to the arrival of Europeans. Among the earliest investigations of archaeological sites along the middle Red River, for example, was an 1897 study of a mound near Campti, Louisiana, by George Beyer of Tulane University. Beyer recovered a ceramic vessel with a design element that he interpreted as a swastika, in his words "that most ancient symbol of good luck and prosperity." He noted: "Of one point . . . we may be assured in connection with this object under consideration, that it is entirely too fine in execution to be ascribed to our North American Indians, but, on the contrary, indicates an introduction of foreign thought and element."[1]

Beyer went on to argue that the earliest mounds were constructed for raising dwellings above swampy lowlands. Eventually, according to Beyer, the mound builders were replaced by ancestors of modern Indian tribes, who were more nomadic and used the mounds only for burials. In these interpretations, Beyer adhered to the nineteenth-century perspective that placed human groups on an evolutionary hierarchy of "progress." Historically known American Indians commonly were assigned to a lower stage than those who were responsible for the mounds and some of the finer artifacts found therein.

This notion effectively was put to rest (at least in scholarly studies) by the work of Bureau of American Ethnology archaeologists in the early twentieth century. Some of the most elaborate earthworks (not just mounds, but earthen ridges in a variety of geometric and animal shapes) relate to the Adena and Hopewell cultures of the Ohio River valley. As dating methods improved, it was clear that these earthworks were constructed as early as 400–500 BC, the beginnings of what archaeologists generally refer to as the Woodland period in the eastern United States.

We now know that the actual start of mound building occurred earlier than Adena and Hopewell—much earlier. Recent research proves that construction of earthen mounds occurred in the 3700–2800 BC interval in northeast Louisiana, a couple of millennia after occupation of the Conly site. The largest and most thoroughly explored site with mounds is the Watson Brake site in Ouachita Parish, which includes eleven mounds on an extensive earthen embankment (fig. 11). Mounds of similar antiquity have been found at several locations in eastern Louisiana and western Mississippi.[2] After a hiatus of about a thousand years, one of the most spectacular mound sites in North America was occupied between about 1730 and 1250 BC. This is the Poverty Point site located in West Carroll Parish along Bayou Macon in northeast Louisiana, now on the UNESCO World Heri-

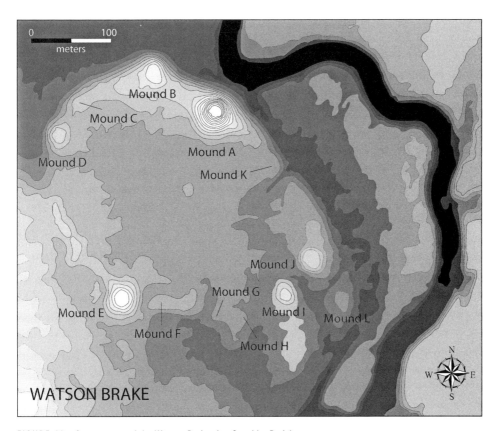

FIGURE 11. Contour map of the Watson Brake site, Ouachita Parish

tage List.[3] The site consists of five mounds and a series of six ridges that form concentric semicircular arcs. Artifacts are abundant at Poverty Point, but we are not certain that shelters or houses were present.

Researchers debate whether Poverty Point represents the center of a regional polity or a trade and/or ritual hub utilized by loosely connected social groups. However, it seems clear that for the time it was unique, and it appears that contemporary earthworks were rare. No significant changes are evident regionally during the early Woodland period, after the demise of Poverty Point. A few possible mounds, but no sites that can be considered substantial ceremonial centers, have been identified. About 100 BC, construction commenced at the famous Middle Woodland–period Marksville site in Avoyelles Parish, eventually an elaborate ceremonial center with earthen berms, conical mounds, one large, flat-topped mound, and a large plaza.[4] However, although a few mound sites contemporary to Marksville are known, other groups do not appear to have developed similar ceremonial centers characterized by multiple earthworks and plazas.

Early Mounds in Northwest Louisiana

Archaic-period people living in the Red River drainage of northwest Louisiana did not construct mounds.[5] However, during the succeeding Woodland period, sometime in the interval between about 500 BC and AD 500, several small, solitary mounds were built on ridges overlooking the Red River floodplain or major tributaries such as Bodcau Bayou. Eight of these have been identified in Louisiana, and three more are present to the north in southwest Arkansas. It is possible that there were others that have been destroyed or have yet to be recorded.[6]

Like the other mounds in northwest Louisiana that date to this period, the Bellevue mound sits on the edge of a ridge directly overlooking extensive bottomlands, in this case the floodplain of Bayou Bodcau in Bossier Parish. The mound is approximately 2 m (6.5 ft) high and 20 m (65.5 ft) in diameter, although earlier descriptions suggest that it might have been slightly larger in the past (fig. 12). During the early 1950s, Robert Fulton excavated a portion of the mound as part of his research for a master's thesis through the University of New Mexico, and he collaborated with Clarence Webb on a report of the work that was published in 1953. Fulton cut a trench through the center of the mound on a north-to-south axis. Fulton's trench went completely through the mound deposits and into the old ground surface beneath. Under the mound was a "sand and clay midden" into which fourteen *postholes* were found in an oval pattern (fig. 13). A shallow pit within this oval contained two partial human cremations, thought to be of an adult and small child.[7] Fulton uncovered a bed of ash adjacent to the pit, and another a few meters away. The lowest mound layer was sandy and covered by a mantle of red clay that ranged from 2.5 cm to 60 cm (1 in to 24 in) thick. The Bellevue people interred an elderly female in a flexed position on the clay platform near two additional beds of ash. They then covered the clay with another thin stratum of earth containing artifacts. To complete the mound, they added a thick zone of sandy fill that lacked artifacts.

Although Fulton and Webb recovered more than seven hundred fragments of pottery, only six were decorated. The decorations pertain to types (Marksville Incised, Churupa Punctated) known to date to the Woodland period. Recovered dart points include the types Gary, Ellis, and Yarbrough. Interestingly, discovery

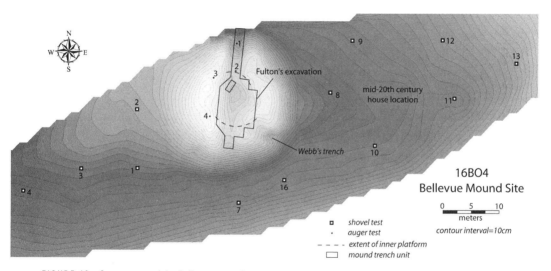

FIGURE 12. Contour map of the Bellevue mound

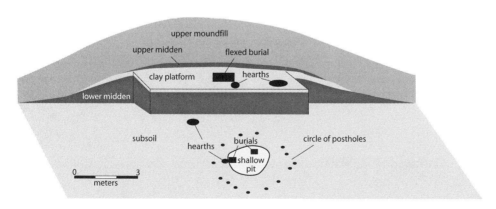

FIGURE 13. Schematic drawing of features in Bellevue mound (*Modified from Webb 1984*)

of two San Patrice points suggests that the site had been occupied briefly thousands of years earlier. Other stone artifacts include a scraper, three *manos,* an unworked quartz crystal, and chipping debris. Fulton and Webb noted that thickly wooded conditions made it difficult to assess how much debris was present in areas around the mound, but there were "some evidences of a thin midden cover several acres along the stream," and they plotted an area of "village refuse" on the northeast of the mound on their site map. We know little, however, about the lifestyles of the Bellevue inhabitants, or those of contemporary people in surrounding areas.

In the summer of 2011, a joint project was carried out by the new landowners, the U.S. Army Corps of Engineers, and the Regional Archaeology Program at Northwestern State University to map the remaining mound and excavate small tests on the adjoining ridge to determine whether associated artifacts and features were present (fig. 14). Fulton's trench, and another reportedly dug by Webb on the southeast side of the mound, had not been backfilled, but the sides were slumped and covered with thick vegetation. We cleared a small portion of the slump and excavated auger holes on the west side of the mound but did not find any remnants of the reported clay platform. We did find a few *potsherds* and some stone chipping debris in the mound fill and from the small excavation units. The Army Corps of Engineers filled in the old trench, cut the trees, and placed a layer of earth over the mound to stabilize it (fig. 15). The Bellevue mound is one of the few that has been restored and is protected.

FIGURE 14. East side of Bellevue mound in July 2011 showing shovel test in the foreground

FIGURE 15. Looking east at the Bellevue mound, November 2011, after restoration

Archaeologists discovered the Coral Snake mound in Sabine Parish prior to construction of Toledo Bend Reservoir in the middle 1960s, a project that resulted in the inundation of about 750 sq. km (186,000 acres) of the Sabine River bottomlands. Although extremely limited in scope given the immensity of the undertaking, attempts were made to inventory and explore a few archaeological sites prior to closure of the dam. In 1965 an archaeological survey crew from the University of Texas mapped and partially excavated a small mound located on a low rise in the floodplain near the mouth of Bayou La Nana. The following year, a crew from Southern Methodist University continued the investigations by digging a trench through the center of the mound.[8]

Underlying the earth used to construct the mound, archaeologists found a basin-shaped depression 6 m (approximately 20 ft) in diameter and up to 1.2 m (4 ft) deep. The Indians later filled the basin and erected a low mound (60–90 cm) (2–3 ft) over the surface. Found within this low mound were fire basins, human cremations, and caches of artifacts (some of the caches included pieces of human bone). The lower mound was capped with sandy deposits, ranging in thickness from 30 cm (1 ft) on the sides to 2.1 m (7 ft) in the center. Within these upper deposits, the Coral Snake people placed several human burials and a fire basin. In total, the Coral Snake mound encompassed ten fire basins, thirty-five human cremations, fourteen *bundle burials,* and fourteen *artifact caches.* The fire basins contained organically stained sand and, in four cases, burned fragments of possi-

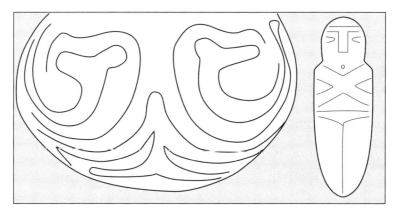

FIGURE 16. Long-necked bird motif on the lower portion of a jar in the style known as Marksville Incised (*left*) and quartz-crystal pendant (*right*) from the Coral Snake mound. (*Original artifacts curated at the Texas Archeological Research Lab, University of Texas at Austin*)

bly human bone. It was not clear if the burning events occurred in place within the mound, or whether the burned deposits and bone fragments had been transported to the mound from elsewhere. Twenty-eight of the cremations were found in the inner mound, one on the surface of the inner mound, and five in the outer mound (the provenience of one was not clear). From the remaining fragments of bone, it was evident that both infants and adults were represented. Buried with the charred bone of one infant were two large stone knives.

The fourteen bundle burials consisted of clusters of disarticulated human bone including two isolated skull fragments, one with copper staining. Only one of these burials contained artifacts—three tubular copper beads. Other artifacts were found scattered in the mound deposits, but some (potsherds and stone chipping debris) may have been accidental inclusions already in the earth used to construct the mound. Likely to have been deliberate offerings were a Marksville Stamped jar, a quartz figurine (fig. 16), a *boatstone,* a copper *gorget,* a copper *pendant,* and eight copper beads. Some of these items were part of artifact caches that the Indians apparently placed on surfaces as they built the mound upward.

Cultural Developments during the Woodland Period

Artifacts found in the areas immediately surrounding these mounds are sparse, suggesting that few, if any, people resided at the sites on a sustained basis. It appears likely that Woodland-period peoples in Louisiana continued the traditional hunting, fishing, and plant food gathering subsistence activities that had sustained groups back to the Paleoindian period. However, some groups, especially those who lived near the Gulf coast in southern Louisiana, formed relatively permanent villages where large amounts of habitation debris accumulated. The abundance of game, fish and shellfish, and plant foods was sufficient to nourish relatively large numbers of people for extensive spans of time at particular places.

Throughout the Woodland period, north of Louisiana as far as the present midwestern states, people increasingly utilized plants with edible oily and starchy seeds. Some of these plants (including erect knotweed, maygrass, chenopod, and sunflower) underwent morphological changes that suggest they were subject to human selection and were planted in gardens—in other words, they became domesticated. Maize already had been domesticated in Mesoamerica by this time, and it apparently diffused, at least in small amounts, into portions of the eastern United States. However, in Louisiana domesticated plants appear to have been of only minor importance, and there is little evidence that they were used at all in the northwestern part of the state. It has been suggested that high labor costs of processing seed foods discouraged their use in areas where other plant foods were abundant and available all year. Nuts (hickory, pecan, acorn) and persimmon continued as important foods in Louisiana, along with fish, deer, and a variety of small mammals.

Although American Indians manufactured and used ceramic vessels and other objects of fired clay as early as the Archaic period (a small number of pottery fragments have been recovered at the Poverty Point site), pottery appears to have been of relatively minor importance until the Woodland period. Prior to about 100 BC, pottery appears to have been most abundant in the southeastern part of Louisiana. By the Middle Woodland period, or between about 100 BC and AD 400, Indians made and used (and broke!) pottery throughout the state, but often only in small quantities. Investigators recovered potsherds within and near the mounds described above. By the Late Woodland period (ca. AD 400–900), pottery was abundant and is found in almost all archaeological sites. Thus, there was a very long span of time between the initial appearance of pottery and its general use. Pottery production is best seen as a gradual technological development rather than an "invention" that spread rapidly from group to group. People knew how to fire clay to make containers and other objects long before clay items became commonplace and nearly ubiquitous across the landscape. Why did the popularity and diffusion of pottery occur during the Woodland period and not earlier, and why so slowly? The increasing use of small plant foods during the Woodland period might have been one critical factor. The Indians began to store small seeds and to develop new food preparation methods such as boiling to make stews. Gardening required concentration of food production at particular places, resulting in less group mobility. Ceramic vessels are cumbersome and easily broken in transit and thus are more likely to be used by sedentary peoples.

Social implications are connected to the manufacture and use of pottery as well. Vessels can be decorated using a wide range of techniques, and artistic styles may mark different dimensions of social status. Archaeologists have used pottery classification and study of spatial distributions as a primary means of identifying and demarcating territories of past social or political groups. Some groups symbolized hierarchical status differences using pottery—for example, especially well-crafted vessels may have been limited to use and display by community leaders. A few styles spread over vast regions and apparently were connected to religious or social ideologies adopted by widely separated societies. For example, burial mounds, exotic ritual objects, and certain styles of pottery (both in form and decoration) suggest that some Louisiana peoples participated in an extensive cultural tradition or interaction sphere known as Hopewell that ranged from the Ohio River valley in the Midwest, across the Lower Mississippi valley and at least as far west as the Sabine River. Incised on one vessel from the Coral Snake mound are a pair of stylized long-necked birds, a common Hopewell design theme (see fig. 16). Items possibly involved in interregional exchange networks include copper ear ornaments and rolled copper beads, stone earspools, platform pipes, ceramic animal effigies, boatstones and celts of exotic material (source areas not known), galena, quartz crystals, and perforated animal teeth. Some of these items, or the raw materials needed to manufacture them, might have come from places as close to Louisiana as the Ouachita Mountains in central Arkansas. Others (for example, copper) likely came from greater distances. The number of exotic items is relatively small, and they have been found only in a few widely dispersed sites. It is not known whether these material connections indicate widespread belief systems or if the objects' shared stylistic features had different local meanings. Why some groups became involved in these extensive stylistic trends, and others did not, is a question of considerable interest to be addressed by future research.

Probably the most easily recognized (and frequently collected) prehistoric artifacts in the United States are stone points, or what are commonly referred to as "arrow points" (fig. 17). Most of these points, however, actually were made and used prior to the development of the bow and arrow, which did not occur until the seventh or eighth century AD. Prior to this time, ranged weapons consisted of short spears (or "darts") tipped with relatively large stone points, either thrown

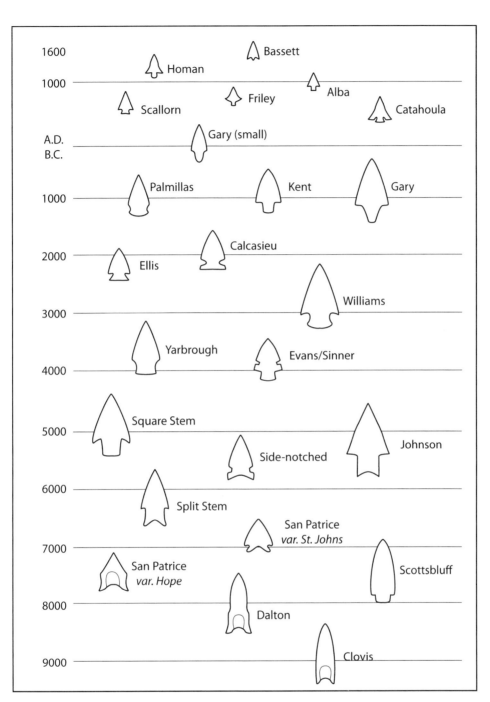

FIGURE 17. General sequence of projectile point forms common in northwest Louisiana

directly or with the aid of *atlatls*. In order to tip arrows shot by bows, however, hunters replaced these relatively large stone points with very small thin ones, generally less than an inch in length and made by shaping flakes that had been removed from larger stone cobbles. Use of the bow and arrow undoubtedly affected hunting strategies and warfare tactics and may have resulted in significant changes in political and economic systems. Another ongoing challenge is to learn more about the timing and implications of changes in stone tool technologies and forms of weaponry.

Early Ceremonial Centers

There is evidence that, during the Woodland period, relative to earlier times, people in northwest Louisiana coalesced and developed more intensive and sustained social relationships with their neighbors. The social landscape became more integrated over larger regions, and this change had implications for human settlement, including the use of mounds. In the last half of the first millennium AD, earthwork construction in Louisiana was no longer sporadic and disconnected—the phenomenon caught on, expanded geographically, and became regionally more complex through time. This trend did not occur in all parts of the Southeast. In fact, the Late Woodland period is sometimes depicted as a sort of Middle Ages (which interestingly occurred at the same time across the ocean) wedged between a classical Hopewell-Marksville period and the Mississippian-period "Renaissance." Like the Old World analogue, however, this perception only makes sense from particular geographic perspectives. In the lower Ouachita, lower Red, and Catahoula basin areas of central Louisiana, a highly complex and dynamic cultural landscape developed during the Late Woodland period.

The largest, most elaborate, and to some degree best-known center of this period is the Troyville site, now completely incorporated within the town of Jonesville. Troyville is situated immediately below the confluence of the Ouachita, Little, and Tensas Rivers, where they merge to form the Black River, a large stream that empties into the Red River near its confluence with the Mississippi. The number of mounds formerly present at Troyville is not known, but at least eight can now be identified, and as many as thirteen were reported in the nineteenth century. The site was extensively damaged by the middle 1930s, when Winslow Walker of the Smithsonian documented what was left, including the remnants of Mound 5, one of the largest earthworks ever constructed in prehistoric North America. It reportedly stood over 24 m (80 ft) high and contained two platforms with a conical mound at the top.[9]

Walker found surfaces of split cane within the lower mound remnant as the fill was removed for use in construction of a bridge over the Black River. In 2006, when the bridge was replaced, the old bridge footing was scraped, revealing some of the wood and cane that came from the mound. Radiocarbon analysis on a sample of the cane yielded a date in the AD 679–778 interval. In his investigations along the highway leading to the bridge, Aubra Lee of Earth Search Inc. identified postholes that appeared to represent at least six circular structures radiocarbon dated to the seventh and eighth centuries. Dates from charcoal obtained from portions of the embankment surrounding the site indicate that construction of the ceremonial center began as early as the sixth century.[10] At least eleven other sites with mounds that appear to have significant components relating to this period are known along the lower Ouachita. However, Troyville was significantly larger in size and, in terms of diversity of earthworks, of greater complexity than other sites, suggesting that it was of primary political, ritual, and/or economic significance prior to the tenth century in the lower Ouachita region.

The westernmost ceremonial center contemporary with Troyville is the Fredericks site, located on a rise overlooking the Black Lake Bayou bottom east of the Red River near Natchitoches. The site contains two mounds of moderate size (Mounds A and C) and three (Mounds B, D, and E) that are low (less than 1 m [39 in] high) and dome shaped (fig. 18). The mounds, along with extensive midden deposits, are situated on a ridge along the bluff edge. During the late 1960s, archaeologists recovered a large collection of artifacts and animal bone from the midden. Only about 5 percent of the more than six thousand recovered pottery sherds are decorated, but design elements are very similar to those on pottery recovered at the Troyville site. In 1997, I directed a field school from Northwestern State University in excavating test units into Mounds B, C, and D (fig. 19).[11] Eight radiocarbon dates on charcoal recovered from within and beneath Mounds B and C suggest that occupation took place within the AD 400–800 range. We found a thin clay platform near the base of Mound C, and both Mounds B and D had clay caps that overlay loamy fill containing human burials. At least two postholes found in Mound B indicate that a structure formerly existed there. However, debris is highly concentrated on the midden ridge, an area that does not appear to be large enough to house a large residential population, and we recovered few artifacts in shovel tests scattered throughout the remainder of the site. Although investigations have been limited, it seems likely that people who lived in surrounding areas congregated for rituals involving feasting and human burial at the Fredericks site.

Establishment of places of public ritual prior to earthwork construction

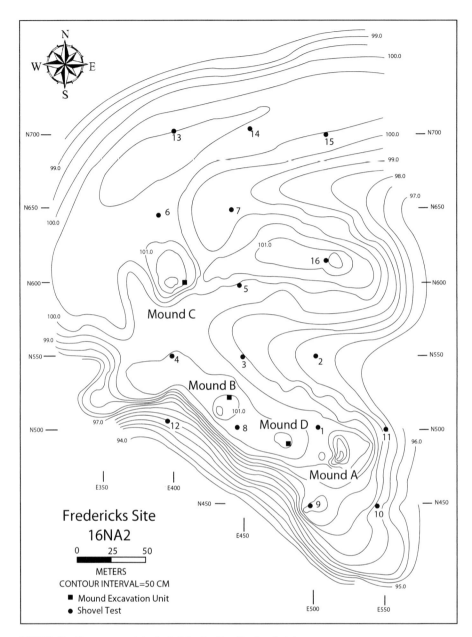

FIGURE 18. Contour map of the Fredericks site, Natchitoches Parish

appears to have been a common occurrence for Late Woodland ceremonial centers, including early occupations at sites such as Mounds Plantation in northwest Louisiana (see below). The impetus for the Late Woodland elaborations was social integration—public ceremony to attract and organize dispersed populations. It is not clear why integration became important at this time. In the central Lou-

FIGURE 19. Students from Northwestern State University conducting excavations at the Fredericks site in 1997

isiana region, there were no apparent links to economic changes such as increasing dependence on farming. It is possible that early use of the bow and arrow might have increased hunting productivity, resulting in population increases, or stimulated aggression, necessitating political consolidation for defense. But, perhaps more important than why the ceremonial center trend started is why it then persisted. Whatever the initial reasons, communities linked by close social and economic ties may have had advantages over smaller, isolated communities in terms of resource and information exchange, increased ability to raid neighboring areas for natural resources or labor, and protection from other groups undergoing similar changes. As some groups consolidated, others were compelled to do likewise or be eliminated as separate systems of organization.

The coordination of construction projects and ritual over an extensive territory would seem to call for strong leaders. But, in contrast to later Mississippian-period, including Caddo, societies, evidence does not indicate that power and prestige were based on, or symbolized by, the possession of sacred or exotic items by individuals. Burials at ceremonial centers were communal and not reserved for political or religious leaders. The mortuary programs at Troyville and other centers show little evidence of differentiation based on status, either of groups or of individuals. Masses of "secondary" interments were placed on platforms later covered by mound fill at locations such as the Greenhouse site in Avoyelles Parish. "Secondary" interments refer to skeletons that have become disarticulated, perhaps from bodies having been placed in *charnel houses* until the soft tissue rotted away, with the bones then moved to another location for burial. At this time, the Indians placed few grave goods in burial areas, although there are exceptions such as two spectacular painted effigy vessels from Gold Mine Plantation in Richland Parish. However, these objects did not appear to be associated with specific individuals but were found within a general dispersed scatter of human bone. In stark contrast to early Caddo mound shaft tombs of the late eleventh and twelfth centuries, the lower Mississippi valley burials lack nonlocal items of copper, marine shell, or knives and effigy pipes of exotic stone. What is clear is that an increasingly interconnected and competitive sociopolitical environment developed in the Late Woodland period in central Louisiana. Northwest Louisiana was relatively isolated from this trend until the late tenth century, a time when mound centers proliferated in the lower Ouachita and lower Red River regions to the south and east, and, slightly later, the immense Cahokia site near present-day St. Louis rapidly developed.

4

BEGINNINGS OF CADDO CULTURE
(CA. AD 900–1300)

They came up from under the ground through the mouth of a cave in a hill which they call *Cha' kani' na*, "the place of crying," on a lake close to the south bank of Red river, just at its junction with the Mississippi. In those days men and animals were all brothers and all lived together under the ground. But at last they discovered the entrance to the cave leading up to the surface of the earth, and so they decided to ascend and come out. First an old man climbed up, carrying in one hand fire and a pipe and in the other a drum. After him came his wife, with corn and pumpkin seeds. Then followed the rest of the people and the animals. All intended to come out, but as soon as the wolf had climbed up he closed the hole, and shut up the rest of the people and animals under the ground, where they still remain. Those who had come out sat down and cried a long time for their friends below, hence the name of the place. Because the Caddo came out of the ground they call it *ina'*, "mother," and go back to it when they die. Because they have had the pipe and the drum and the corn and pumpkins since they have been a people, they hold fast to these things and have never thrown them away. From this place they spread out toward the west, following up the course of Red river, along which they made their principal settlements. For a long time they lived on Caddo lake, on the boundary between Louisiana and Texas, their principal village on the lake being called *Sha' childi' ni*, "Timber hill."[1]

In the late nineteenth century, anthropologist James Mooney recorded this Caddo origin story during his study of the Caddo people in Oklahoma (fig. 20). Almost all societies have traditional origin stories connected to religious beliefs and rituals. Rather than being narratives of physical events of the past similar to those of modern academic pursuits such as history and archaeology, they convey spiritual truths. The purpose is to pass along through the generations a sense of cultural identity, how people are connected to one another, and how they are connected to nature.

FIGURE 20. *Caddo Creation Legend*, by Acee Blue Eagle (*Northwestern State University of Louisiana, Watson Memorial Library, Cammie G. Henry Research Center, Caroline Dormon Collection*)

What do we mean when we refer to the "beginnings" of a culture from a material perspective? It is unlikely that the American Indian people of northwest Louisiana at any particular point recognized that they were forming a "new" way of life that constituted a fundamental break from the past. In retrospect, however, modern researchers can identify critical changes that occurred during the ninth and early tenth centuries in terms of settlement patterns, economic factors, social connections, and artistic styles for which we can trace continuities into historic times. We thus look upon that time as the commencement of the Caddo cultural tradition with the recognition that there is no specific date or event marking the transition.

The initiation of Caddo culture was not an isolated phenomenon that can be understood solely in terms local to northwest Louisiana. Changes were part of a widespread pattern that transpired throughout much of what now constitutes the southeastern and midwestern United States. Archaeologists refer to this as the transition from the Late Woodland period to the Early Mississippian period. Interconnections intensified between societies, resulting in widespread similarities in economic, political, and ideological behaviors. A critical interval in the formation of the Mississippian world was the development of the awesome Cahokia site in an area known as the American Bottom—a broad zone where the Illinois, Missouri, and Mississippi Rivers come together. It is an area that has been extensively studied by archaeologists, not only because of the spectacular nature of what remains there but also due to long-term research that was conducted prior to a highway project that eventually destroyed peripheral portions of the site. The ancient city of Cahokia (one of the largest residential and ceremonial centers in the world at that time) covered 16.8 km² (6.5 mi² or more than 1,618 ha [4,000 acres]), of which 60 ha (150 acres) were within fortified walls (fig. 21). The people of Cahokia built mounds—lots of them. Between 100 and 120 mounds have been identified at the site, and many more were once located where the cities of St. Louis and East St. Louis now are situated. During the period from about AD 1050 to 1250, the Cahokians created and inhabited a huge metropolis, approximately 13 km (8 mi) long and containing more than 200 mounds.[2]

At the center of Cahokia is Monks Mound, the largest earthwork north of

FIGURE 21. *Central Cahokia*, by Lloyd K. Townsend (*Courtesy of Cahokia Mound State Historic Site*)

Mexico. The mound, which still stands, is about 305 × 259 m (1,000 × 850 ft) in extent, with the upper platform rising 30.5 m (100 ft) above the surrounding land surface. It is estimated that it contains 622,970 m³ (22 million ft³) of earth (all basket-loaded). One of the more intriguing aspects of Cahokia is the presence of large circular arrangements of upright wood posts known as *woodhenges*. Although we do not know for certain, many archaeologists believe that the woodhenges were used like giant sundials to mark the summer and winter solstices and other calendrical events.

There is evidence that Cahokia was ruled by a very powerful group of people. Excavation of one of the mounds (known as Mound 72) revealed twenty-five burial pits containing at least 272 individuals. With some of the burials were numerous grave goods, many of nonlocal materials including high-quality stone, and minerals such as copper and mica. One person was buried on a layer of more than 20,000 shell beads—the shells were from marine animals and probably came from the Gulf of Mexico. Some of the burial pits contained many individuals—as many as fifty-three were in one pit. In one burial, investigators found masses of arrow points neatly grouped by different outline forms.

To some archaeologists, the Mississippian tradition began here and spread to other areas in the Southeast and Midwest. Others, however, see Cahokia only as the most spectacular outcome of cultural events that were ongoing across vast regions, perhaps triggered by the advent of a new economic pattern—a pattern that involved intensive food production (including maize agriculture) in floodplain settings of major river valleys. Other explanations involve the development of widespread networks of trade and exchange of information, as well as warfare, greatly expanding and intensifying interactions between formerly separated regions. None of these ideas are mutually exclusive, and it seems likely that all contributed to the character of the time period that we refer to as "Mississippian."

Let us take a look at what happened in northwest Louisiana during this very interesting era.

Mounds Plantation: An Early Ceremonial Center

Montroville Wilson Dickeson, born in Philadelphia in 1810, was a doctor, taxidermist, and avid collector of fossils. Between 1837 and 1844, he pursued another interest—excavating American Indian burial mounds in the Ohio and Mississippi River valleys. He claimed to have "opened up" more than a thousand mounds and collected more than forty thousand objects. He also made drawings of the mounds and later provided these to an artist by the name of John J. Egan, who, about 1850, converted the drawings into a series of large paintings on huge canvases. Dickeson toured the country in 1852, allowing the public to view the canvases and his artifact collections for a fee of twenty-five cents. The *Panorama of the Monumental Grandeur of the Mississippi Valley* was 2.3 m (7.5 ft) high and 106 m (348 ft) long, and consisted of twenty-five scenes. The canvases later were curated at the University Museum, University of Pennsylvania, until 1953, when they were purchased by the St. Louis Art Museum, where they remain today. The museum also has copies of Dickeson's lecture notes in which he described Scene 21: "The following picture shows a group of connected mounds in Caddo Parish, in Northwestern Louisiana, with some of the aboriginal inhabitants of the region."

Scene 21 depicts a cluster of nine mounds, some of which are connected by low earthen walls. In the background are mountains, and a group of Indians with elaborate headdresses are shown in front of tents (fig. 22). Similar mountains and the same Indian scene appear in other segments of the Mississippi panorama and are understandable in light of the Romantic artistic style of the times, as well as the fact that the panorama was part of a show intended to evoke wonder and awe in its audience.

Today we know of only one place in Caddo Parish where there is a cluster of at least nine mounds. Located on the western side of the Red River, north of the present city of Shreveport, is the Mounds Plantation site, the single largest Caddo

FIGURE 22. John J. Egan, *Panorama of the Monumental Grandeur of the Mississippi Valley* (scene 21 of 25), ca. 1850, distemper on cotton muslin; original of all twenty-five scenes is 90 in × 348 ft (*Courtesy of Saint Louis Art Museum, Eliza McMillan Trust 34:1953*)

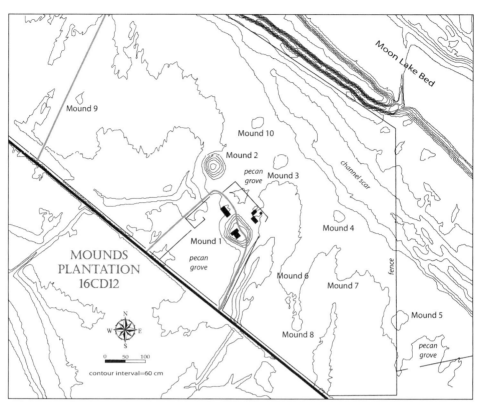

FIGURE 23. Topographic map of the Mounds Plantation site in Caddo Parish

ceremonial center in northwestern Louisiana (fig. 23). It seems fitting that the earliest reference that we have to a prehistoric site in northwest Louisiana likely pertains to Mounds Plantation, a place of primary importance to its ancient Caddo inhabitants, as well as to modern archaeological research. Dickeson apparently visited Mounds Plantation not long after Henry Shreve initially cleared portions of the Great Raft between 1833 and 1838. His reference to Caddo Parish suggests that his visit took place in or after 1838, the year that the parish was formed. Logjams that left much of the floodplain under water continued in northern Caddo Parish until the final clearing of the raft in 1873. The 1839 survey plat for that area shows that the site would have been situated on the margin of an extensive floodplain lake, known as Soda or T'Soto Lake, which may be depicted in Egan's painting. We also suspect, however, that portions of the site were inundated for long periods of time. Floodwaters deposited a layer of clay that overlies the old surface upon which we find Caddo artifacts.

Two of the mounds at Mounds Plantation (Mounds 1 and 2) are well preserved and remain very large. Two others (Mounds 3 and 5) also were quite large until

1959, when the landowner removed tenant farmhouses that had been placed on their summits and began to cut the mounds down to incorporate the deposits into his cultivated fields. As this work proceeded, he encountered human bone and contacted a local rancher named Ralph McKinney, who had an interest in American Indian history. McKinney supervised as his workers excavated a trench through Mound 3 and later made extensive excavations into Mound 5. Clarence Webb made periodic visits while the work was ongoing and took notes about the findings.

We recently placed several small excavations adjacent to Mound 2 and through the remnant of Mound 6. We encountered postholes and midden areas, indicating that the site was inhabited prior to construction of the mound and plaza complex, and radiocarbon dates reveal that this occupation took place during the late tenth and early eleventh centuries. There is little evidence of contemporary sites in the area, and it may be that most of the regional population was concentrated at Mounds Plantation. Too little research has been undertaken to provide a firm chronology of events, but it is apparent that by the twelfth century, at least some of the mounds began to be constructed, and the site increasingly became a center for ritual activities. Webb found a dense concentration of animal bone and some curious earthworks beneath Mound 3, and he interpreted these as possibly related to rituals involving large communal feasts. Similar kinds of remains have been found beneath other early Caddo mounds, indicating that it was a common practice to construct mounds over areas once used for rituals. Subsequently some of the mounds may have served as platforms upon which the Indians built structures of special religious or political function—although no postholes or other direct evidence for this have been found at Mounds Plantation. We do know, however, that in at least one mound, Mound 5, the remains of deceased community leaders were interred. Special mortuary treatment of community leaders might date back to the Woodland period as described in chapter 3. However, Caddo practices, like those in many contemporary Mississippian-period societies, differed greatly from previous times.

Prior to the eighteenth century, the Caddos commonly interred their deceased leaders in large burial pits sunk deeply into mounds. These pits are often referred to as "shaft burials." Most individuals were lined up in one row, sometimes with others perpendicular to the row at the heads and feet. Although orientations vary, placement on a southwest-northwest axis was the norm. Men, women, and children are all represented in the burial pits. The Caddos sometimes placed a few items (personal ornaments such as bead necklaces or bracelets, ear ornaments, wood-covered copper rattlers, and clusters of arrow points) directly with specific individuals, but most items were deposited in clusters along one side (generally the side opposite the heads of the primary row of individuals) or in the corners of the pits.

The reasons for placing several individuals in the same pit are not known. Individuals buried in mounds are likely to have been the social or religious leaders of the community. The inclusion of men, women, and children suggests that high status was conferred on entire families rather than specific individuals. Webb suggested three possible reasons for burial of multiple individuals in the same pit: (1) death in warfare; (2) epidemics; and (3) human sacrifice. He argued that the latter is most likely, given the absence of supporting evidence for the first two. The fact that the Caddos at this time lived in dispersed settlements and did not construct fortifications suggests that warfare was not a major concern. Epidemics would have resulted in large numbers of contemporary burials in village areas, something not found in Early or Middle Caddo period contexts. Human sacrifice was practiced by some southeastern groups, such as the Natchez, in historic times. Family members and servants were sacrificed upon the death of a preeminent leader. As information from the Gahagan site suggests, however, in some cases it also is possible that, although several individuals wound up together, all were not buried at the same time (see below).

We have two spectacular examples of how early Caddo people buried their leaders. The burials inform us not only about burial practices but also about Caddo society, trade with other peoples, artistic accomplishments, and religion. The first place we will examine is Mound 5 at Mounds Plantation. The second was located near the small community of Gahagan in Red River Parish. The Gahagan site, or most of it, washed into the river during the 1940s, but excavations in one mound were made prior to that unfortunate occurrence.

Mound 5 at Mounds Plantation: A Special Mortuary

In 1959, the former landowner of Mounds Plantation removed the upper two-thirds of the western portion of Mound 5; he took additional fill from the top of the eastern portion in the following year and uncovered bone fragments and broken pottery, suggesting that a human burial was disturbed. In the fall of 1960, McKinney was allowed to excavate remaining portions of the mound. Webb participated intermittently and made notes, photographs, and drawings.

Near the top of the mound (within the upper 50 cm [20 in]), McKinney encountered two burials, both with ceramic vessels that, like those from the Mound

3 burial, probably date to the seventeenth century, long after most of the site had been abandoned. After finding these burials, the investigators excavated four trenches into the mound (fig. 24). Although the situation was not completely clear, it appeared that the mound was constructed in at least two stages. There was no evidence of midden accumulation or soil development on top of the inner, primary mound, which was approximately 1.2 m (4 ft) high. However, the Caddos had placed several large burial pits into the mound. Burial Pit 6 probably was the earliest. It extended through the primary mound and contained seven individuals placed in a row with heads to the southwest. Above their heads were three additional individuals with heads to the northwest. Included in the pit were several smooth stones, bone pins, and a cluster of twenty-five arrow points. Six other burial pits (Burial 4 and Burials 10 through 14) also were placed in the primary mound. These pits contained between one and three individuals and had

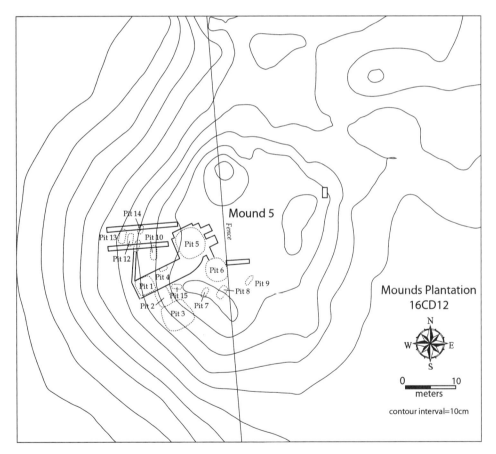

FIGURE 24. Excavations in Mound 5 at the Mounds Plantation site

few grave goods. Near the southwestern edge of the mound, a layer of sand and clay capped the primary mound. Through this, Burial Pit 1 intruded and contained a row of five individuals with a sixth individual placed perpendicular on the north side about 20 cm above the base of the pit.

After the Caddos added a second mound stage, they sunk a large (4.6 × 4 m, or 15 × 13 ft) central shaft burial (Burial Pit 5) through the mound into the underlying deposits. The pit contained twelve individuals along with numerous burial goods (fig. 25). Several well-preserved logs overlay the burials. Two radiocarbon determinations on samples taken from these logs relate to the twelfth century AD. The burials in this pit were segregated into five groups. Group 1 consists of a single adult male and two children whose remains were only partially preserved.

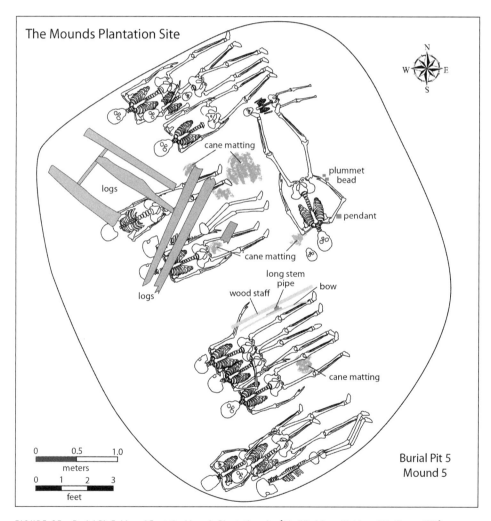

FIGURE 25. Burial Pit 5, Mound 5, at the Mounds Plantation site (*Modified from Webb and McKinney 1975*)

The adult was interred in a distinctive position with his arms and legs slightly bowed outward. Individuals buried in similar positions have been found at other contemporary mound centers elsewhere in the Caddo area, most notably at the George C. Davis site (Caddoan Mounds State Park) in Texas and at the Crenshaw site in Arkansas. The position is similar to that of what appears to be a dancing figure depicted on ornaments at several Mississippian sites, particularly a marine shell cup from the Spiro site in Oklahoma. The figure appears to be wearing a feathered cloak and has a raptorial, birdlike beak. It may be that certain political or religious leaders in early Caddo societies were dressed as this "birdman" figure prior to burial, and perhaps wore these items while living at certain rituals.

Most of the artifacts from Mound 5 were found in Burial Pits 1 and 5. Included were clusters of arrow points, celts, large stone knives (known as Gahagan knives after the Gahagan site), various other stone tools, a few wooden implements in-

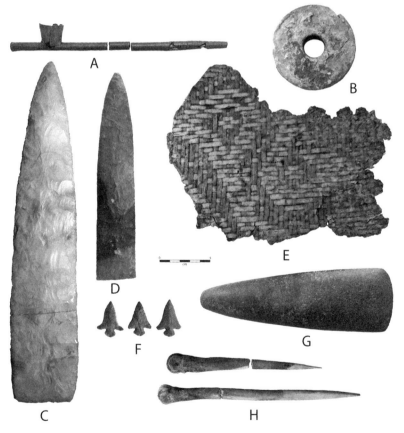

FIGURE 26. Artifacts from the Mounds Plantation site: long-stem ceramic smoking pipe (A); copper-covered stone ear ornament (B); large stone knives known as Gahagan knives (C, D); split-cane matting with bird-head design (E); Homan arrow points (F); polished stone celt (G); polished bone awls (H)

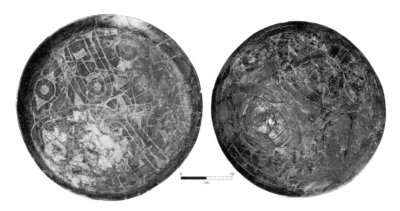

FIGURE 27. Engraved bowl from Mound 5 at the Mounds Plantation site

FIGURE 28. Designs on engraved bowl from Mound 5 at the Mounds Plantation site

cluding fragments of two bows, split-cane mats, and a few pottery vessels (fig. 26). One of the vessels is decorated in a way that is unique in the Caddo area, although a few vessel fragments with somewhat similar design elements have been recovered in the Cahokia area (figs. 27 and 28). The bowl was engraved on both the interior and exterior. The interior is separated into four zones within which are eye symbols. The bowl decorations represent an early example of Mississippian iconography, which would become more widespread and elaborate through the fifteenth century elsewhere in the Southeast.

The Gahagan Burial Mound and Connections to the Mississippian World

The first archaeological investigations in northwest Louisiana that provided considerable data for future research were conducted by Clarence B. Moore in 1911 and 1912. Under the auspices of the Academy of Natural Sciences of Philadelphia,

Moore traveled many of the major waterways of the Southeast in a steamboat named the *Gopher.* Between the city of Alexandria, Louisiana, and the Arkansas state line, he investigated twelve sites, including Mounds Plantation (referred to as "Pickett's Landing"), Byram Ferry, Cedar Bluff, Thompson, Sunny Point, and Gahagan. Moore focused on mounds, particularly those with human burials and accompanying grave goods, and described his findings in a series of well-illustrated reports that have recently been reprinted.[3] Although his excavation methods and descriptions of the mound sediments do not approach the quality of later twentieth-century investigations, the illustrations and descriptions of artifacts continue to be of major research importance. Many of the sites that he described were destroyed or badly damaged by erosion and agricultural activities shortly after his investigations.

One of the most interesting sites Moore investigated was located in Red River Parish along Honey Bayou near the small community of Gahagan (fig. 29). In 1912 he observed, "In aboriginal times a considerable population must have inhabited this place, to judge from the number of remnants of mounds that are scattered throughout the fields." He conducted excavations only in the largest mound, subsequently designated Mound A. By 1938, Clarence Webb and Monroe

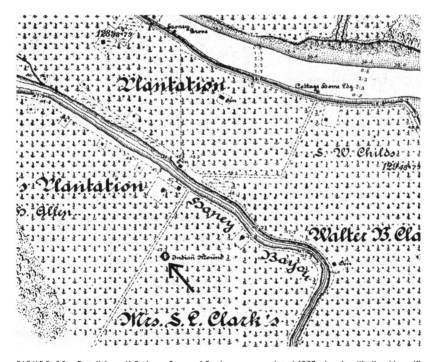

FIGURE 29. Detail from U.S. Army Corps of Engineers map, dated 1887, showing "Indian Mound" south of Honey Bayou (*U.S. Army Corps of Engineers, Vicksburg, Miss.*)

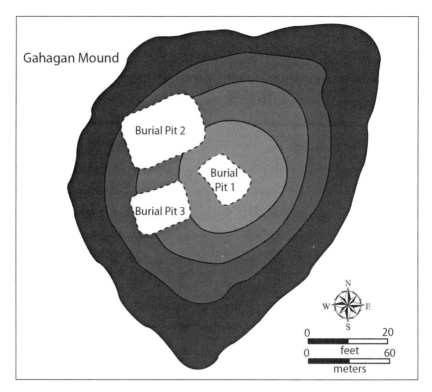

FIGURE 30. Location of burial pits in Mound A at the Gahagan site

Dodd noted only Mound A, two low rises (Mounds B and C), and numerous circular sandy areas that contained pottery when they conducted additional investigations at Gahagan. Mounds B and C might have been small constructed earthworks that capped structures. Webb and Dodd excavated two more burial pits in Mound A before the mound was destroyed by a change in the course of Red River (fig. 30).

Moore described Mound A as being composed of clay and sand. Although partially eroded and plowed, it was slightly over 3.3 m (11 ft) high and an estimated 24 × 33.5 m (80 × 110 ft) in extent. He dug into the center of the mound through a large 13 m² (144 ft²) burial pit (Burial Pit 1) that extended to 3.3 m (11 ft) below the summit. Skeletal remains of five individuals were found in the pit along with several ornaments and stone tools located near the head of the central individual (fig. 31). Additional ornaments, containers, and tools had been placed in clusters along the northwest side of the burial pit.

The largest tomb, Burial Pit 2, was filled with a "charcoal-streaked red clay and sand mixture." The pit dropped 2.4 m (8 ft) from the summit and had a level floor of white and yellow sand. At the base were the skeletal remains of six individuals

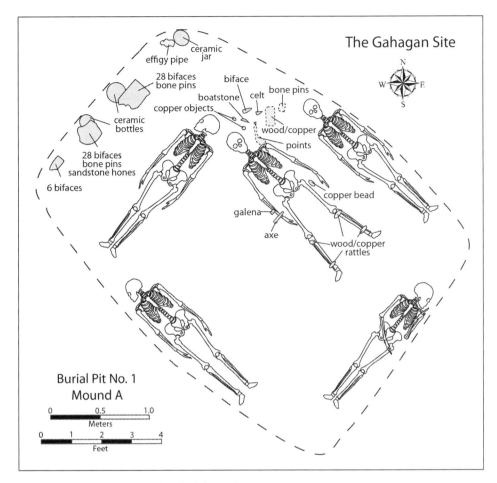

FIGURE 31. Burial Pit 1 in Mound A at the Gahagan site

placed in a single row with heads to the northwest, with one exception oriented in the opposite direction (fig. 32). A seventh individual was placed perpendicular to the others. Artifacts associated with the individuals were sparse, consisting only of copper-covered stone or wood ear ornaments and two caches of arrow points. As in Burial Pit 1, however, in the northwest edge of the pit the Caddos placed multiple clusters of items including many of the distinctive stone knives now known as Gahagan knives or bifaces. Some of the more interesting items were a human effigy pipe made of stone, two human hand effigies of sheet copper, and two long-nose god masks made of copper. Radiocarbon dates later were obtained from organic material attached to three of the objects from Burial Pit 2. The dates indicate that the burial relates to the late eleventh or early twelfth century AD.

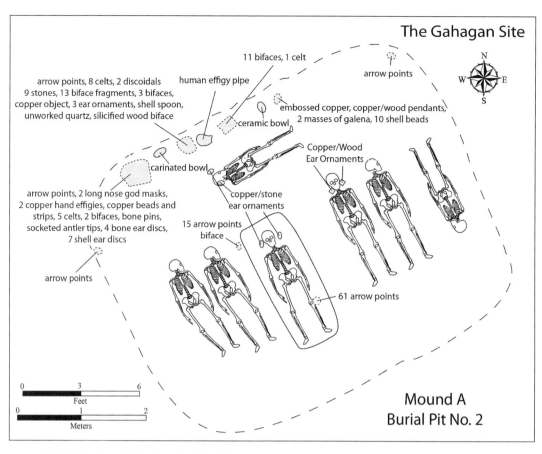

The Gahagan Site

11 bifaces, 1 celt

human effigy pipe

arrow points

arrow points, 8 celts, 2 discoidals
9 stones, 13 biface fragments, 3 bifaces,
copper object, 3 ear ornaments, shell spoon,
unworked quartz, silicified wood biface

embossed copper, copper/wood pendants,
2 masses of galena, 10 shell beads

ceramic bowl

Copper/Wood
Ear Ornaments

carinated bowl

copper/stone
ear ornaments

arrow points, 2 long nose god masks,
2 copper hand effigies, copper beads and
strips, 5 celts, 2 bifaces, bone pins,
socketed antler tips, 4 bone ear discs,
7 shell ear discs

15 arrow points
biface

arrow points

61 arrow points

0   3   6
Feet

0   1   2
Meters

Mound A
Burial Pit No. 2

FIGURE 32.   Burial Pit 2 in Mound A at the Gahagan site

In Burial Pit 1 at the Gahagan site, the central individual is the only one with
associated items (rattles, galena, axe, and possibly a cluster of items near the
head). A person in a similar position (with legs and arms in the "birdman" con-
figuration) was present in Burial Pit 2. Numerous artifacts (copper-covered stone
ear ornaments and a cache of sixty-one arrow points by the left knee) were associated with this individual, undoubtedly a person of particularly high status,
perhaps the paramount community leader. Webb noted that a separate pit intruded into the fill of the original pit, and the burial was not quite at the same
level as the others, suggesting that the individual was interred at a later time.
The intrusive pit did not disturb earlier burials, and the orientation and placement in the row of the individual was close, but not identical, to the other interments. When the original group were buried, a gap must have been left specifi-
cally for this person. We do not know how much time elapsed, but knowledge of
the location of the gap must have persisted. A gap also is present in the central

row in Burial Pit 1, possibly representing a space intended for an individual that, for some unknown reason, never occupied it. Burial Pit 3, investigated by Webb and Dodd, was smaller, approximately 3.7 × 3.4 m (12 × 11 ft). The depth and fill reportedly were similar to those of Burial Pit 2. The pit contained a row of three individuals with heads to the northwest (fig. 33). As in the other burial pits, most artifacts were placed along the northwest margin. The eastern portion of the pit was empty, again perhaps intended for persons not yet deceased who never were placed there.

Copper artifacts are found very rarely in Caddo archaeological sites. There are no local sources of copper in or near northwest Louisiana, so the Caddos must have obtained these items through trade with groups in the Midwest (particularly Cahokia) or with other southeastern peoples who had access to copper. The graves in the mound at Gahagan contained many finely crafted ornamental items

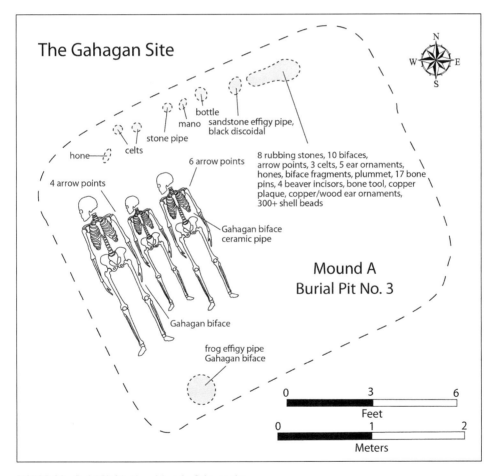

FIGURE 33. Burial Pit 3 in Mound A at the Gahagan site

of copper, including two long-nose god maskettes, a cut-sheet copper human hand symbol, and embossed copper ear ornaments pressed onto both cypress wood and stone (fig. 34). Other items include copper-covered wood and stone ear spools, a second sheet-copper hand symbol, copper-covered wood beads, copper-plated marine shell fragments, cut strips of sheet copper, rolled copper cylinder fragments, and polished bone ornaments with copper staining. The presence of these items denotes the importance of rare and exotic items in early Caddo society—as sacred symbols relating to increasingly widespread religious beliefs in the Midwest and Southeast, or as emblems of the social, political, or religious status of the deceased individuals that they accompanied in the tombs.

Among the unusual items found at the Cahokia site in Illinois, but interestingly not found in burials, are *effigy figures* made from a distinct soft, red stone called CBP Missouri flint clay. Chunks of this stone that apparently represent debris resulting from manufacture of the effigies have been found at the site as well, all in contexts that date to the early twelfth century. Tom Emerson of the University of Illinois conducted tests demonstrating that the stone used to make these figures came from the Ozark Mountains just south of St. Louis, Missouri. He performed the tests using a device called a portable infrared mineral analyzer, or

FIGURE 34. Copper items from the Gahagan site: long-nose god maskette; copper-plated wood ear ornaments; cut-sheet copper hand symbol (*Items in Webb Collection, Louisiana State Exhibit Museum, Shreveport*)

PIMA. It is a short-wave, infrared, reflectance spectrometer that produces a visual printout of infrared spectra of the constituent elements of the stone. The analysis is based on the fact that different minerals absorb infrared light in different ways and the relative proportion of different minerals in the claystone are unique to different source areas.

Archaeologists have found similar effigy figures elsewhere in the Southeast, including two at Gahagan—a beautifully carved frog holding a ceremonial rattle (fig. 35) and a crudely made image of a kneeling man (fig. 36). In 2002, Emerson analyzed the two Gahagan effigy pipes using the PIMA device. He found that the proportion of minerals in the Gahagan effigies was identical to that found from the specimens at Cahokia and concluded that the Gahagan frog and man were made from Missouri flint clay found only in the Ozarks south of St. Louis—thus, the specimens likely were made at Cahokia and traded into the Caddo area. But when?

FIGURE 35. Frog effigy pipe of Missouri Flint Clay from the Gahagan site (*Item in Webb Collection, Louisiana State Exhibit Museum, Shreveport*)

FIGURE 36. Human figure pipe of Missouri flint clay (*Item in Webb Collection, Louisiana State Exhibit Museum, Shreveport*)

Emerson initially suggested that the figures were moved into the Caddo area many years after they were made and used at Cahokia, when their value at Cahokia declined and newly complex societies formed to the south during the thirteenth century. A problem was that, based on pottery styles, Louisiana archaeologists have traditionally thought that the Gahagan site dates earlier than this by at least one hundred years. But we had no dates. Webb and Dodd did their work prior to the advent of radiometric dating techniques, which were developed during World War II and began to be widely used in the 1950s. As noted earlier, radiocarbon dating works only on organic materials that contain carbon—former living things, plant and animal remains, not on stone or pottery. Fortunately, some of the objects recovered from the Gahagan burials are made of wood and leather (and partially covered with a thin layer of copper) and amenable to radiocarbon dating. Since this technique is destructive, we did not want to use the objects themselves to obtain dates. However, small portions of the wood and leather had become detached over the years that the objects have been in storage, and recent improvements in radiocarbon dating techniques (AMS methods) now enable us to date very small amounts of organic remains. We analyzed three samples of crumbled material, and the results strongly suggest that the pipes were brought to Gahagan in the twelfth century at the pinnacle of cultural developments at Cahokia rather than later as initially hypothesized by Emerson. Many archaeologists now believe that the presence of the massive Cahokia polity likely was one factor in the early development of the Caddo cultural tradition.

Understanding the possible ways that peoples in northwest Louisiana interacted with those at Cahokia and other areas in the Southeast is one of the most fascinating topics in archaeological research. Frank Schambach, formerly of Southern Arkansas University, suggested that the exotic objects associated with the distinctive Early Caddo period burial program came into the Caddo area through trade relationships with Cahokia. He argued that the Caddos might have sent prized bows made from the wood of bois d'arc or Osage orange to the North in exchange for ritual items (and knowledge). Why the figure pipes and copper items were buried at Gahagan, and not at larger contemporary ceremonial centers such as Mounds Plantation, is a mystery. Given the challenge of transporting people and goods across the vast intervening territory (remember, no horses or wheeled vehicles at this time), it is not likely that Cahokians exacted tribute, posed military threats, or levied direct economic influence on the Caddos. However, visitations, pilgrimages, trading expeditions, and other forms of social interaction undoubtedly took place. The acquisition and ritual display of exotic items became important for establishing and maintaining leadership positions in

Caddo society. Movement of people, information, and goods between northwest Louisiana and Cahokia stimulated new social and political arrangements in both regions and connected people of the Caddo area to the increasingly integrated Mississippian world in eastern North America. In chapter 5 we take a closer look at Caddo society as it developed during the ensuing centuries.

5

ORGANIZATION OF THE CADDOS IN PRECOLONIAL TIMES (CA. AD 1300–1700)

Cultural developments that took place in northwest Louisiana in the twelfth and thirteenth centuries had important implications regarding the organization of Caddo groups when first encountered by Europeans during the late seventeenth and early eighteenth centuries. Of particular importance was the growth of dispersed villages along secondary streams in the Red River floodplain. Increasing dependence on maize agriculture as a subsistence base likely was an important factor in this change in settlement. New burial practices, particularly for community leaders, signify important social and political reorganization. The Caddos also altered their arrangement of mounds and ceremonial activities across the landscape and made adjustments in trade practices and other interregional interactions.

As noted previously, Mounds Plantation developed into a large ceremonial center with a substantial residential population by the twelfth century. There is little evidence of nearby settlements in the Red River floodplain. However, on the east side of the river, in a pasture a few miles south of the present town of Benton in Bossier Parish, the remains of a substantial habitation area were found buried almost 2 m (6 ft) below the present surface. Little of the site has been investigated, but pottery and radiocarbon dates indicate that people lived there during the early (pre-mound) occupation of Mounds Plantation (by the ninth century). At a later time, probably beginning in the twelfth century, when the ceremonial center across the river had been created, the Caddos established a few households downstream along a stream that is now known as Willow Chute Bayou. Between about AD 1200 and 1450, a time for which there is little evidence of occupation at Mounds Plantation, these households joined to form an extensive village.[1] It is possible that some of the former Mounds Plantation residents and their descendants moved southeast and helped establish the Willow Chute community. The layout of the community differed markedly from Mounds Plantation. No longer did people aggregate at a single center with residences surrounding a vast mound and plaza complex. They now were strung out in dispersed villages made up of small clusters of houses with associated agricultural gardens and perhaps small outbuildings that served as storage shelters. This pattern continued along the Red River into historic times, as seen in a depiction of a Caddo settlement upstream along the Red River made in the winter of 1691–92 during a Spanish expedition led by Domingo Terán de los Ríos (fig. 37). The drawing probably is of the upper Nasoni Caddo village and shows multiple clusters of small farmsteads, each containing several buildings, ramadas for shelter, and above-ground granaries. A single mound is depicted with a structure marked "Temple" at its summit.[2]

Spanish missionaries during the eighteenth century reported that the Caddos of East Texas had a special temple area that served as the residence of the Grand Xinesi, or paramount leader, who presided over a large territory comprising several local communities (later referred to as a "confederacy" by ethnohistorian John Swanton). Although the Xinesi appears to have been held in considerable respect in religious terms, he wielded little actual political power. Lesser centers might have been associated with the groups constituting the confederacy, and these centers contained the residences of local leaders, the Caddi, who, along

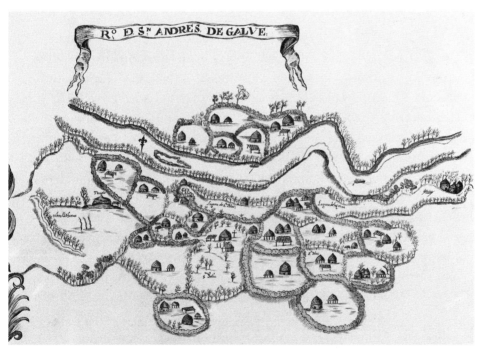

FIGURE 37. Detail from Terán map of a Nasoni Caddo village, 1691 (J. P. Bryan Map Collection, di_09638, Dolph Briscoe Center for American History, University of Texas at Austin)

with a council of elders (Canahas) made most community decisions. It has been assumed that the groups along the Red River were organized in a similar manner, but few historic descriptions of these peoples were written during the eighteenth century or earlier, and our information is very limited.[3] Let's take a closer look at the Willow Chute community.

A Dispersed Village along Willow Chute Bayou

Over the span of almost a decade, Louis Baker, a local amateur archaeologist, discovered and made repeated surface collections at more than fifty archaeological sites along Willow Chute Bayou in Bossier Parish. Most of the areas suitable for prehistoric settlement were recently in cultivated fields with excellent surface visibility, but many have now been obscured by residential construction. I worked with Baker for several years recording additional sites and analyzing the artifact collections that he had amassed. A permanent village along Willow Chute appears to have started at the north end of the stream, where a relatively large settlement, known as the Festervan site, was found buried beneath almost 2 m (about 6 ft) of alluvium in places. Radiocarbon dates indicate that it was occupied from the ninth to the eleventh centuries, contemporary with the early occupation at Mounds Plantation, which is located a short distance to the north on the west side of the river. Expansion of population downstream along Willow Chute occurred by the late twelfth century, eventually forming a dispersed village consisting of multiple clusters of houses similar to those depicted on the Terán map. Communication within the area would have been easy as all sites are within a half day's walk—a total length of about 12 km (7.5 mi) along contiguous well-drained natural levees. From what we know about general changes in pottery styles and from radiocarbon dates at a few sites, it appears that the community flourished until the early fifteenth century.

As it is today, Willow Chute Bayou likely was an abandoned course of the Red River at the time of the Caddo occupation. Geological studies suggest that by about 2,000 years ago, the natural levees along the stream appear to have been essentially stable, suggesting that the main channel of the Red River was in its modern course to the west by that time. The area probably was at a higher elevation than natural levees along the active channel during the Caddo occupation, leaving it free from major episodes of flooding and bank caving. Eventually, however, as a ridge of alluvium accumulated along the modern course of the Red River, the propensity for flooding along Willow Chute increased—a possible reason for abandonment of the area. By the early nineteenth century, Willow Chute was an uninhabited backswamp, and a layer of clay or silt loam now covers most of the archaeological sites. Artifacts found by Baker were exposed along the slopes to the bayou after deep plowing, but larger portions of the sites were discovered on surfaces buried between 30 and 60 cm (12 and 24 in) below the present surface.

Excavations at one site revealed the presence of postholes, indicating that houses were once present. Spanish missionaries in the eighteenth century described Caddo houses as being shaped like a cone or "beehive" (fig. 38). This style of house appears to date back to the earliest Caddo villages. Where sufficiently large areas are excavated, archaeologists often find postholes in circular arrangements, usually with a large posthole and hearth in the center. The circles (and presumably the houses) generally range between 5 and 12 m (16 and 39 ft) in diameter. It is believed that the Caddos placed upright, vertical posts in small holes (the postholes later identified by archaeologists) dug at equal distances from a large central post. They then drew in and tied the tops of the posts together, forming a cone-shaped framework. Horizontal braces were attached to the posts, and

FIGURE 38. Reconstructed Caddo house that formerly stood at Caddoan Mounds State Historic Park near Alto, Texas

FIGURE 39. Postholes found at the Vanceville site in Bossier Parish. Fill has been removed from the example on the right.

the structure was thatched with thick grasses and split cane. The builders cut out the central post and fashioned a hearth where it formerly stood. These houses likely burned easily and frequently, often leaving circular charred remnants of the vertical posts that we find in our excavations (fig. 39).

The Caddos eventually constructed at least three mounds in the Willow Chute locality. Two, the Vanceville and Swan Lake Mounds, are small (about 2 m [6.5 ft] high) and conical in shape. They are surrounded by artifacts, and postholes have been found at both sites. Although neither mound has been excavated, artifacts recovered in the surrounding areas do not differ significantly from those recovered elsewhere along Willow Chute, and there seems to be no reason to believe that the presence of the mounds was linked to high social status for the Vanceville residents relative to their Willow Chute neighbors. As at Mounds Plantation and Gahagan, the mounds may contain burials of community leaders.

The Werner site, located near the southern edge of the Willow Chute locality, included a mound and evidence of a structure that differ considerably from those found at the Vanceville and Swan Lake sites. The landowner leveled the mound during the early 1930s. When Clarence Webb visited in 1936, he noted that the

FIGURE 40. Aerial view of the excavations at the Werner Mound in Bossier Parish (*Webb 1983*) (Reproduced by permission from the Oklahoma Archeological Survey, University of Oklahoma)

mound had been approximately 38 m (125 ft) in diameter and reportedly was taller than the Vanceville Mound (fig. 40).[4] The fill was red, sandy loam, similar to the surrounding deposits, and no evidence of burials or other cultural features was noted. Local Boy Scouts, partially supervised by Webb, excavated the former mound area during 1958 and 1959 and uncovered a floor of "packed, level, red clay" with post molds and two ash pits. Most of the post molds were arranged in two concentric circles. The outer circle was approximately 24 m (79 ft) in diameter and the inner circle approximately 14 m (46 ft) in diameter (both significantly larger than typical Caddo houses). On the eastern side of the larger circle, the pattern bulged out to form what appeared to be an elaborate entrance. Although the possibility was considered that the outer ring represented a corral, probable roof- and wall-construction materials (burned small timbers, daub, and cane) were found along a portion of the arc, leading Webb to conclude that a large structure with an inner chamber was represented.

Little habitation debris was present in the immediate vicinity of the mound, and the artifacts that were recovered are atypical for the Willow Chute area. The Werner site contained an unusually high percentage of potsherds, many exhibiting highly polished surfaces with red and white pigments in the engraved lines. Chipped stone tools and chipping debris, common at other Willow Chute sites, were present only in small quantities. The excavators also recovered numerous cut and perforated mussel shells (possible ornaments). The faunal assemblage was skewed to the presence of bones that would have yielded choice meat cuts, particularly of deer. These traits suggest that the structure beneath the Werner mound was not a typical habitation locus but may have served as a meeting place for community leaders or a place of religious or ritual significance. A radiocarbon analysis from one of the postholes suggests a mid-fifteenth-century date for the structure. Apparently, the Caddos erected the mound to cover the remains of the structure, perhaps one of the last events that took place in the Willow Chute community.

We do not know much about the nature of the ceremonies that occurred at the Werner site, but Spanish missionaries in the eighteenth century observed rituals carried out by the Hasinai Caddo groups in East Texas. It was noted that the Hasinai held feasts several times a year, with both community members and neighboring groups often participating. Community leaders (Caddi and Grand Xinesi) were honored and presented with gifts. According to Father Casañas, "For three days and nights the feast goes on with dancing, eating, and fun." Father Espinosa described some of the ritual activity connected with the feasts:

> It is at night during the new moon in September. The first night the crowd of old conjurors, medicine men, captains, and necessary officials and servants spend within doors. The rest who come lodge outside by families where they build a fire for light as well as because the cold is already beginning to be felt. After two of the old men say their prayers between their teeth, they stand for more than an hour, take tobacco—as well as bits of meat—and throw it on the fire which is in the middle of the house. Then they sit down on their benches and all the old men and captains are given the rest of the meat. They mix with it their drink of brewed wild olives which is served them three or four times in an earthenware vase. They take pipes of tobacco which they pass around to everybody. . . . At midnight a crier begins to call all the families in their order. They come in by threes, one woman from each house, and each presents a pot or small vessel of very fine meal and some rolls which they call *bajan* made of a thick paste of roasted corn and the seed of sunflowers. The majordomos then deposit these in two big receptacles of their own. In this way the criers continue to call and all the houses and families make their gifts. This finished, the offering is divided among the old men, the captains, and officials of the settlement.[5]

Mounds Plantation (discussed in chapter 4) probably continued to serve as a regional ceremonial center during the initial expansion and early development of the Willow Chute community, but it appears that substantial residential occupation at the site ceased by the mid-thirteenth century. Regional ceremonial centers may have continued to exist upstream in the Red River floodplain at sites such as Haley and Mineral Springs in southwest Arkansas. However, the dispersion of population from Mounds Plantation appears to mark a major shift in Caddo social organization in northwest Louisiana. Although many people continued to live in the Red River floodplain after AD 1200, they were not integrated by a single large ceremonial center as was the case earlier. Possible reasons for the change from the relatively aggregated settlement pattern include: (1) subsistence practices—the Caddos increasingly relied on maize agriculture; (2) demographics—population levels increased, triggering territorial expansion; (3) social fragmentation—it became difficult to maintain a single social hierarchy for the increasingly large and dispersed population.

Scattered sites have been identified along Cowhide Bayou, Red/Stumpy Bayou in north Caddo Parish, and Red Chute Bayou in southern Bossier Parish. These bayous are abandoned channels representing older courses of the Red River and are flanked by extensive natural levees that would have been relatively free from the frequent flooding and bank caving that occurs closer to the river. The secondary streams would have contained sufficient flowing water for human consumption, acquisition of riverine food resources, and transportation. We have not carried out enough research, however, to identify the kind of contiguous site distributions evident along Willow Chute. As is the case in the Willow Chute area, perceptions of Caddo floodplain habitation are significantly affected by sedimentation processes. Natural levee surfaces upon which the Caddos lived in many portions of the Red River floodplain are buried by a silty clay overburden revealing only limited numbers of artifacts brought to the present surface by plowing.

Not all Caddos lived in floodplain villages. In fact, most sites dating after AD 1200 are located along upland streams. We do not fully understand the nature of these upland settlements, but they appear to be small and dispersed. It is possible that they were relatively independent of one another, but it also is possible that multiple settlements were integrated into communities similar to those in the floodplains. The absence of mounds and other evidence of ceremonial centers in the uplands suggests that they may have been rural settlements with political, religious, and economic ties to floodplain communities. Much more research is warranted.

Additional work also is needed to learn about how different communities were connected to one another to form more extensive social or political units. During the eighteenth century, Spanish and French colonists identified several "tribal" groupings of related communities (see chapter 6). Assessing social and political landscapes based solely on archaeological data, however, poses considerable challenges. The degree to which Caddo and other American Indian organization as observed in the eighteenth century extends back before written records is unknown. The stability and temporal depth of specific "tribal" groups are questionable. Early twentieth-century researchers assumed that (1) these groups maintained their coherence far back into the past; (2) each produced a distinct archaeological record, particularly with regard to the way they constructed and decorated their pottery; and therefore (3) by identifying the material culture associated with particular groups for the eighteenth century, we can trace their histories back in time as earlier sites are found. We now see that cultural groups are often more like clouds—not distinct, well-bounded entities. Human groups are constantly undergoing transformation—they merge with other groups, break apart, sometimes not completely, and re-form in different ways. Groups may be linked economically but not politically; they may share religious beliefs but be bitter enemies, or a single group can be highly diverse in many of its customs and beliefs. Although these complications may be especially evident in large, relatively complex societies, we often underestimate the multifaceted and dynamic nature of smaller-scale situations. Some times and places are like skies filled with thin, wispy clouds where it is not possible to identify specific groups. Perhaps this is especially true for the earlier periods (particularly Paleoindian and Archaic) where connections were ephemeral between local groups who did not hold specific territories. The bottom line is that the fallout of material culture from the actual flow of history is not as tidy as we initially assumed. These circumstances do not preclude interpretation of social and political organization in the past. They do mean, however, that identification of bygone groups entails more than simple classification of material culture and mapping its distribution across the landscape.

Houses and Human Burials at the Belcher Site

In the early 1930s, a farmer near the town of Belcher in north Caddo Parish cleared an area along Cowhide Bayou and encountered what would turn out to be one of the most significant archaeological finds in Louisiana. As he attempted to level a rise with a slip, he encountered a human skeleton. Fortunately, he continued work in the surrounding area and left the rise alone. In 1936, Clarence

Webb of Shreveport heard of the find and began a project that was to continue for more than twenty years. When Webb first saw it, the rise appeared to be a single earthwork, approximately 2.4 m (8 ft) high and 24–30 m (80–100 ft) in diameter. A low earthen platform extended 12–15 m (40–50 ft) to the northwest. Later the rise was found to consist of two distinct mounds as well as the platform. The bayou and a drainage ditch to the east were slowly eroding the mounds and platform. In 1936 Webb excavated trenches on the east and northeast edges of the higher southern mound and identified two distinct layers of earth with artifacts.

During the fall of 1936, thinking that Webb was done, the landowner made a second attempt to level the mound. This time he encountered a burial with numerous pottery vessels. Webb was contacted and, working on weekends over the course of the next five years, he and his assistants excavated most of the northern mound and platform areas. In 1950, using power equipment, the landowner lowered the southern mound to the level of the adjoining field, using the displaced deposits to fill a drainage ditch. Two years later Webb returned to search for pos-

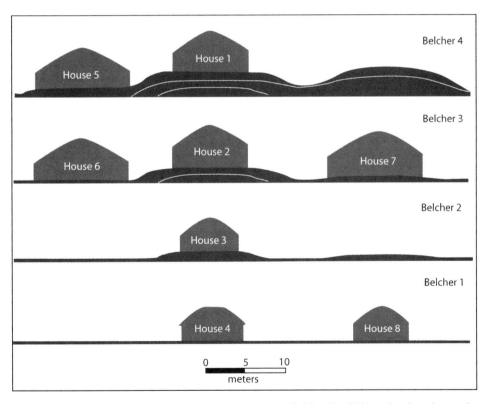

FIGURE 41. Sequence of houses and mound construction at the Belcher site. Webb assigned numbers to the houses as he found them. The central mound was excavated first, with House 1 at the top, House 2 in the underlying layer, and so on.

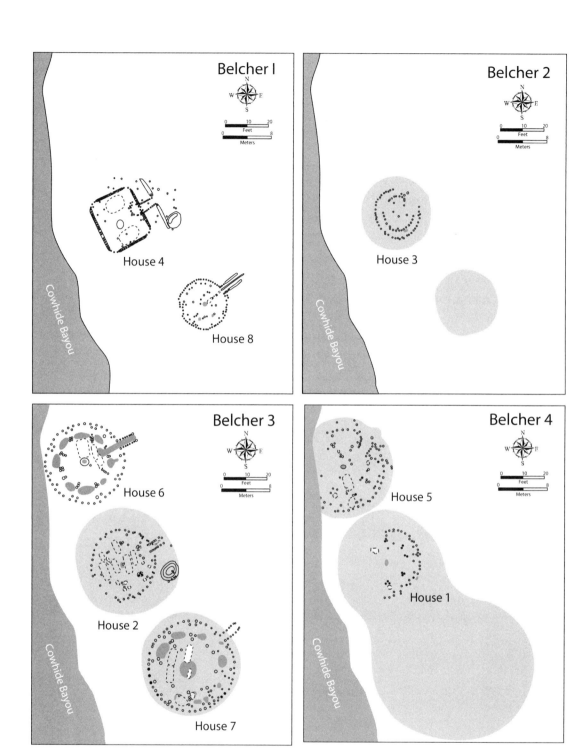

FIGURE 42. Sequence of houses in plan view at the Belcher site (*Modified from Webb 1959*)

sible remaining features. He found that much of the mound was still intact, and another two years of fieldwork ensued. The investigations at the Belcher mound provide the most complete picture of the sequence of events relating to construction and use of a prehistoric mound from the Caddo area. The site is also important because it was occupied over a long span of time. The mound was constructed in layers, resulting in stratified deposits that enabled archaeologists to understand the sequence of pottery changes for the region. Until recently, it also provided the only substantial information on prehistoric Caddo architecture in northwest Louisiana (figs. 41 and 42). Webb's report, published in 1959, is detailed, very well illustrated, and contains a major synthesis of Caddo culture history.[6]

The mound area, and probably a residential zone to the south, were initially occupied at the same time that the Willow Chute community was inhabited. As with many other Caddo mounds, the area appears to have been designated a sacred place prior to construction of the mounds. Postholes found on the old land surface beneath the mound indicate that a rectangular building once existed there (fig. 43). The posts had been set in shallow trenches with a low clay wall or

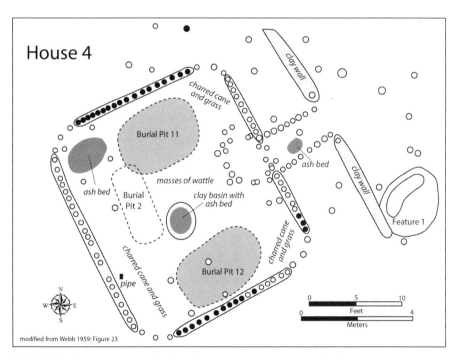

FIGURE 43. House 4 at the Belcher site. Burned postholes are shown in black; unburned postholes are white. Burial Pits 11 and 12 were associated with the house; Burial Pit 2 intruded from an overlying layer. (*Modified from Webb 1959*)

FIGURE 44. Ceramic smoking pipe found along the southwest wall of House 4 at the Belcher site (*Item in Webb Collection, Williamson Museum, Northwestern State University of Louisiana*)

berm adjacent to each trench. On the northeast side, two parallel sets of postholes represented an extended entrance to the structure. A small bed of ashes was present within this passage. Another ash bed was in the center of the structure, and a third was found in the western corner. Also in the center was a concentration of *wattle and daub*. Charred cane and grass were also found in the corners of the house. A large clay pipe was one of the few artifacts found within the structure (fig. 44). Radiocarbon analysis of charcoal from the house indicates that it was built sometime between AD 1295 and 1398.

The structure eventually burned, perhaps as a ritual act by the site residents following the death of an important leader or leaders. A layer of sand was placed over the charred structural remains, and two deep pits (Burial Pits 11 and 12) were sunk into the sand and through the former floor of the building. Each of these pits contained several human burials. One pit extended almost 1.8 m (6 ft) beneath the floor. The skeleton of a male was found in the center, flanked by two adult females and two children. Three pottery vessels, bone tools, and a pipe similar to the one found on the house floor had been placed on the edges of the burial pit. The second burial pit was not as deep and contained three adult females and one child. The pattern of these burials, with multiple individuals in rows and artifacts placed on the sides of pits, is similar to the burials at the Mounds Plantation and Gahagan sites, suggesting an Early Caddo–period affiliation. However, a radiocarbon assay on charcoal from House 4 dated slightly later, in the AD 1295–1398 interval, and much of the recovered pottery from the house also suggests that it dates after AD 1200.

Probably a short time after the burials were placed in House 4, a large circular house (House 8) was constructed to the south, in the area that would eventually become the southern mound. Like House 4, there was an extended entrance to

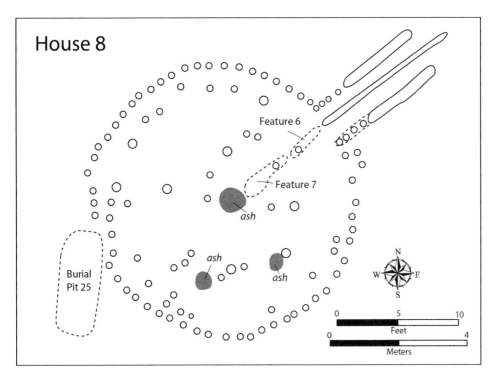

FIGURE 45. House 8 at the Belcher site (*Modified from Webb 1959*)

the northeast. A series of postholes along the wall on the interior may represent supports for a bench or beds (fig. 45). Three ash pits were found within the house, including one in the center. Few artifacts were found, and although the house was burned and capped with a layer of sand, no burials were excavated into its remains.

The sandy layers placed in both areas were later covered with layers of clay. Upon the clay cap overlying House 4 was a structure (or two?) (House 3) consisting of two concentric rings of postholes (fig. 46). The inner ring was slightly oblong, about 4.5 × 4 m (15 × 13 ft). No burning of the posts was evident, but charring was visible between postholes. Webb thought that the outer ring (about 6 × 6.7 m, or 20 × 22 ft) represented a slightly older structure. He did not identify an extended entrance, but several burial pits from the overlying layer intruded into portions of the house, obscuring the deposits.

The next stage (Belcher 3) of development was the most elaborate, with the construction of three houses—two (Houses 2 and 7) on the clay caps over the earlier houses, and a third (House 6) on a low platform to the north. All three houses exhibit similar characteristics, which were best preserved in House 6 (fig. 47).

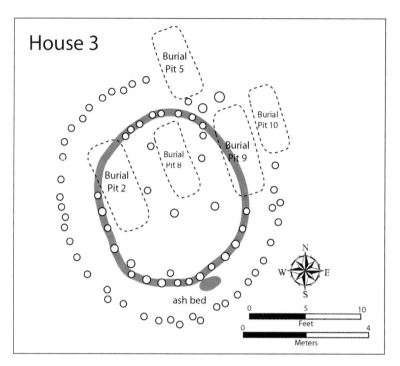

FIGURE 46. House 3 at the Belcher site (*Modified from Webb 1959*)

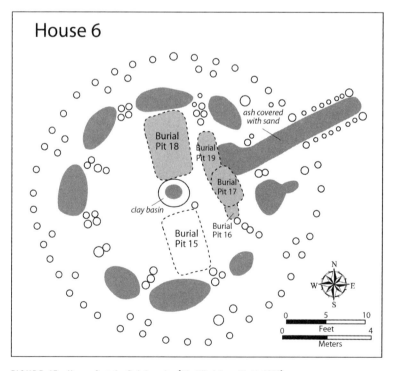

FIGURE 47. House 6 at the Belcher site (*Modified from Webb 1959*)

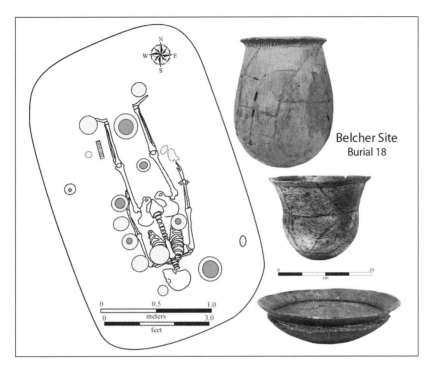

FIGURE 48. Sketch of Burial 18 at the Belcher site with selected vessels: Belcher Ridged (*top*), Foster Trailed Incised (*middle*), Belcher Engraved (*lower*) (*Modified from Webb 1959; vessels are in Webb Collection, Williamson Museum, Northwestern State University of Louisiana*)

The inside of the house was divided into eight areas, each marked by pits containing ash and clusters of three or four postholes. Pairs of postholes found between the ash pits may have supported benches. A basin of fired clay containing white ash was present in the center of the house. An extended entranceway to the house was formed by a shallow channel that was filled with loose sand, covered with ashes, and capped by a layer of yellow sand. All three houses were circular, burned, and had burial pits dug through the deposits capping them.

Most of the burials associated with the Belcher 3 structures had only one to three individuals per grave. Typical is Burial 18 dug through House 6. A single female was in the burial pit. She was surrounded by twelve ceramic vessels (a variety of bowls, jars, and bottles), shell beads, a shell hoe and spoon, a perforated ceramic disk, and bone ear spools (fig. 48).

Demolition and burial of Houses 2 and 7 resulted in the conjoining of the north and south mounds into a single earthwork. It is possible that another house was built on the south portion covering House 7, but if so, traces of it were destroyed when the top of the mound was leveled prior to Webb's investigations.

However, houses were placed atop House 2 on the north mound, and atop House 6 on the platform to the north. It is not clear whether these two houses existed at the same time. House 1, on the north mound, was partially destroyed by plowing but appeared to be another circular structure. No trace of a northeast entranceway was evident. Internal clusters of burned postholes were suggestive of the bench features represented in the Belcher 3 houses. Much charred cane, timbers, and daub were found within the structure, as was a central ash area. Several pottery vessels were found crushed in place on the house floor, but no burials were interred at this stage.

The outer part of House 5 was identified by a floor of packed sand and clay. The house was quite large, probably 11–11.5 m (37–38 ft) in diameter, and had a clay ramp on the northeast but no projecting entrance formed by postholes (fig. 49). However, several small postholes appeared to form an inner entranceway.

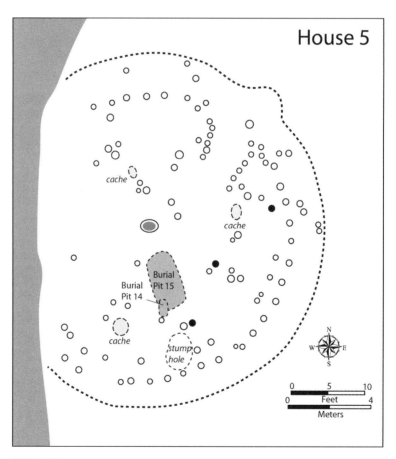

FIGURE 49. House 5 at the Belcher site. Dashed line indicates the extent of the packed clay floor (*Modified from Webb 1959*)

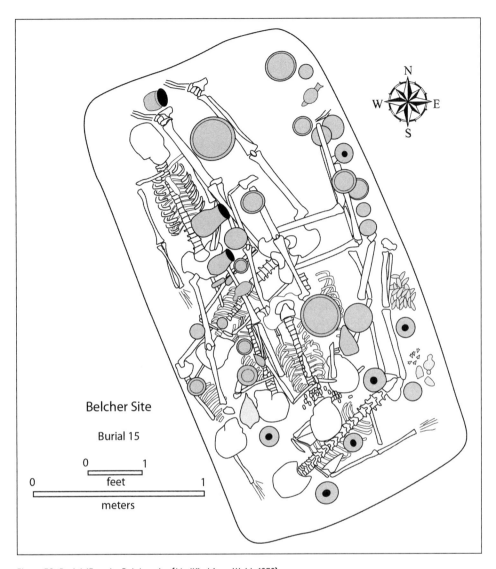

Figure 50. Burial 15 at the Belcher site (*Modified from Webb 1959*)

The structure had a central ash pit in a clay-lined basin. One burial (Burial Pit 15), the most unusual at the site, intruded through the clay house floor. The burial pit was almost 1.5 m (5 ft) deep and contained seven individuals, thirty-three pottery vessels, nine projectile points, a celt, three shell cups, twenty-three shell beads, three pearl beads, one shell pendant, fourteen other shell ornaments, and a mass of garfish scales. Unlike the other burials at the site, the individuals appear to have been thrown carelessly into the pit, with one person face down (fig. 50). In contrast, the artifacts were placed very carefully.

Through time, the Caddos built at least eight houses and placed twenty-six burial pits (containing the remains of at least forty-seven individuals) in the mound area at the Belcher site. No more than three houses existed at the same time. The houses had elaborate features (ash pits, sand-filled entranceways, internal postholes) and contained artifacts not typical of Caddo structures found elsewhere in the region. The structures clearly were special places possibly serving as loci for religious ceremonies, as council houses, as habitations for elite members of society, or some combination of these. Deceased persons placed in the burials likely were the social or religious elite of the community. The fact that men, women, and children are represented suggests that high status was placed on entire families rather than specific individuals. The reasons for placing several individuals in one grave have been the subject of much speculation, but are not known (see chapter 4). Radiocarbon analyses indicate that the houses were occupied and the mound accumulated during the sixteenth and early seventeenth centuries. Although it is likely that the Caddos were using the Belcher site when the De Soto expedition passed by the region in AD 1540, there is no evidence that the Spaniards visited the site or nearby areas. Pottery types that appear to date after ca. 1685 are not present at Belcher, and the site was probably abandoned in the latter half of the seventeenth century for unknown reasons.

Where did the people who constructed the Belcher mound live? Some apparently resided approximately 1 km (.6 miles) downstream along Cowhide Bayou, where Webb identified a concentration of pottery and stone chipping debris. When we reexamined the area in 1995, treasure hunters had disturbed the deposits, but we found pottery dating back to the time of the earliest use of the mound. A cluster of houses was probably present in this area, with others dispersed along nearby secondary floodplain streams. Slightly later sites, located near the downtown airport in Shreveport and in southern Bossier Parish, might represent descendants of Belcher people. These sites probably relate to the Yatasi and Nakasas villages identified by the expedition of Henri de Tonti in 1690, and by Jean-Baptiste Le Moyne, Sieur de Bienville, in 1700.

6

CADDOS AND COLONIALS
(CA. AD 1700–1760)

It was not a pleasant journey. On March 22, 1700, twenty-two Canadians and three American Indians (two Taensa and one Ouachita) led by Jean-Baptiste Le Moyne, Sieur de Bienville, began a westward trek from the Taensa village on Lake St. Joseph in the Mississippi River valley.[1] After crossing a few large rivers, they met a group of Ouachita Indians in canoes loaded with salt who were on their way back to the Mississippi River. The following day, the two Taensas also returned to the east. In his journal, Bienville stated: "The Taensa have deserted me on account of the bad roads and the severe cold. They do not like to wade naked through water."

The party then crossed a river (reported to be full of "crocodiles") at the end of a prairie and passed through a waterlogged country—"A man of medium height is at a great disadvantage when going into such country: I see some of my men in water only up to their waists, whereas I and others are almost swimming, pushing our bundles before us on logs to keep them from getting soaked." On the 26th they found a place to camp: "I stayed at this hunting ground, where my men went out and killed three deer and twelve very fat turkeys. Two of my men have had a seizure of dysentery accompanied by very violent colic." Two days later they arrived at a camp of the Ouachita Indians, which was situated on a large river, or a branch of that river (probably the Ouachita River somewhere south of present-day Monroe). The camp consisted of five huts and about seventy men. The journey continued on March 30, led by a Nadchito guide, and additional Nadchitos were met on their way east to sell salt to the Coroas.

The Bienville expedition continued for several days after crossing the Ouachita, encountering additional swampy land and thick canebrakes. It continued to rain: "Several of my men were so seized with chills in the water that they climbed into trees to get some relief. Four stayed in trees nearly all day—until we sent a raft for them. Never in our lives have my men and I been so tired. . . . We do not stop singing and laughing, as we wish to show our guide that fatigue does not distress us and that we are men different from Spaniards."

On April 6 they came upon two huts of the Natchitoches and arrived at the village of the Souchitionys on the following day. The rest of the Natchitoches reportedly lived about a league away in huts scattered along the Marne River (undoubtedly what we now call the Red River). At the Souchitiony village, women were pounding corn and "the men came for me and carried me on their shoulders underneath a kind of sheltered market-place, roofed with palmetto palms, where they had assembled to sing the calumet to me. I gave a small present to them and to the chief of the Natchitoches, and gave them a calumet of peace. At this village of the Souchitionys there are fifteen huts assembled in a cluster."

The Souchitionys are a group later known as the Doustioni who probably lived along the lower reaches of the Saline Bayou near present-day St. Maurice (fig. 51). Four days later, rather than visiting the Natchitoches who were living along the Cane River channel to the west, the expedition continued upstream in pirogues provided by the Indians. Conditions forced them to abandon the boats and walk overland for a few days. However, on April 15, they came to a large lake, which they crossed with a pirogue made by the French and some additional Indian pirogues that they found. On the far side of the lake were high hills covered with small stones. The next day they arrived at the fifteen-hut village of the Nakasas, which was mostly covered by floodwaters, forcing the inhabitants to camp on constructed platforms. Archaeologist David Kelley investigated archaeological sites in southern Bossier Parish near the community of Ninock that probably represent a portion of this village. The McLelland site was excavated prior to being destroyed by an access road for Lock and Dam No. 5 of the Red River Waterway. Within a myriad of postholes uncovered by the excavations, two circular structures can be discerned (fig. 52). The structures are only about 1 m (3.3 ft) apart and might not have existed simultaneously. North of the structures was an area containing large amounts of chipping debris from the manufacture of stone artifacts, as well as animal bone and plant remains. Finished arrow points were found in the immediate vicinity of the structures. Food remains indicated that corn, beans, and squash were cultivated and consumed at the site along with native seed-bearing plants such as chenopod, sumpweed, and sunflower. Recovery of numerous nut shells indicate that nuts (hickory, pecan, acorn) were of major importance to the Caddos' diet. Deer was the primary source of animal protein, but a wide range of terrestrial and riverine fauna were exploited. Seven human burials were found scattered throughout the site rather than clustered in a cemetery area. The McLelland site was a small farmstead occupied through sev-

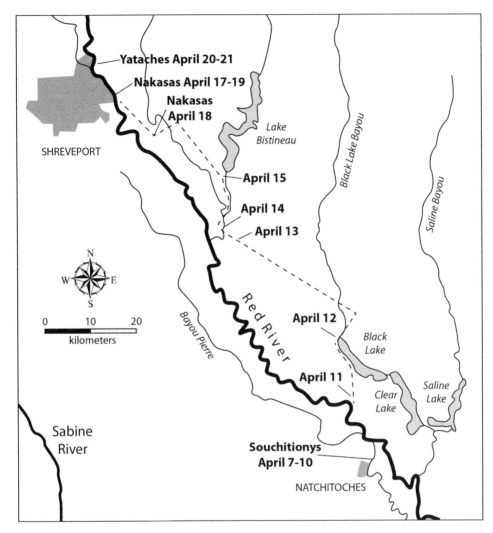

Map labels:
Yataches April 20-21
Nakasas April 17-19
Nakasas April 18
Lake Bistineau
Black Lake Bayou
Saline Bayou
SHREVEPORT
April 15
April 14
April 13
N
W E
S
0 10 20
kilometers
Red River
Bayou Pierre
April 12
Black Lake
April 11
Saline Lake
Clear Lake
Sabine River
Souchitionys April 7-10
NATCHITOCHES

FIGURE 51. Reconstruction by David Kelley of the probable route taken by Bienville from the Natchitoches area to the Yatachez village, April 1700 (*Modified from Kelley 1994*)

eral generations, perhaps by a single extended family. Although, other than one small fragment of copper or brass, nothing was recovered that points to a visit by Bienville or any other Europeans, Caddo villages tended to consist of dispersed habitations and farms rather than tightly clustered residential zones, and it is likely that the McLelland site relates to a portion of the community through which Bienville passed.

On the night of April 17, Bienville's expedition stayed at another village of the Nakasas, this one with eight huts: "Around these huts there is not one arpent that is not flooded. The water is falling noticeably. I found very little corn, owing to

Burial 5

Burial 7

Burial 3

POSSIBLE
RAMADA

Burial 6

Burial 1

Burial 2

Burial 4

STRUCTURE 2

STRUCTURE 1

0   5

meters

FIGURE 52. Pattern of postholes and other archaeological features at the McLelland site (*Modified from Kelley 1994*)

some Yuahes that came visiting here and took away all the corn their horses could carry. . . . All Indians here are tattooed around the eyes and on the nose and have three stripes on the chin." Bienville noted that this village was located on the left, presumably west, bank of the Red River. Perhaps due to subsequent changes in the course of the river, no corresponding archaeological remains have been found, but this village was probably somewhere between the modern port facility and residential areas of southeast Shreveport.

The party continued upstream on April 20 to the village of the Yataches in "two old pirogues, the ends of which were made of clay." Bienville states in his journal: "About two o'clock in the afternoon, I made my way to the Yataches. All their huts are scattered along the river for a distance of 2 leagues. Upon our arrival, the Indians hid their pirogues and corn, because they had learned from an Indian who got there a little ahead of us that we wanted pirogues and food. I threatened to remain with them if they did not give me pirogues and corn for the journey to the Cadodaquios." The next day, "when the Indians led me to believe that they would give me provisions and pirogues, I sent—to get quicker action— one man into each hut with glass beads and other trifles to persuade them to pound corn at once; and I took two with me in one pirogue to make a search for other pirogues all along the river. I could find only three, which I bought for two axes each. Today the water has fallen 2 feet. I have gone inside forty different huts along this river."

We are fairly certain that the Yatache (or Yatasi, as later rendered) village was scattered between the present-day downtown airport of Shreveport and portions of the old Beene Plantation near the intersection of Highway 3 and Interstate 220. During the late nineteenth century, Mr. T. P. Hotchkiss sent artifacts to the Smithsonian Institution that reportedly came from a large burial ground found at a depth of 5.5 m (18 ft) along a cutoff in the Red River. Included were pottery vessels that we now can firmly date to the late seventeenth or early eighteenth centuries. In the 1940s, a scatter of broken artifacts was found in plowed fields on the Beene Plantation to the east. This pottery also consists of specimens that relate to that time. More recently (in 1990) on the Shreveport side (but in Bossier Parish because of an early twentieth-century change in the course of the river), a utility trench intruded into a dark layer of earth 1.8 m (6 ft) below the surface near the downtown airport. Artifacts similar to those found to the east were collected from this dark layer by a local landowner prior to the trench being refilled. I have examined these, and they also date to roughly the time of Bienville's and Tonti's visits. Unfortunately, none of the French "glass beads and other trifles" have come to light.

Bienville was told by the Yataches that it took ten nights to get by river to the ultimate destination, the villages of the mighty Cadodaquios. Bienville believed that the journey would be only two days by land, and his party set out to the northwest on April 22. However, "I came to the decision to break of[f] the journey and return to the ships because I have no more than twenty days remaining of the time specified for me to get there and because I have several men weakened by diarrhea and dysentery, brought on by the cold water and the poor food."

The Bienville expedition was not the first European excursion to Caddo territory.[2] Bienville was retracing the route of the then-elderly French (actually an Italian in the employ of France) explorer Henri de Tonti, who had ventured west from the Mississippi Valley a decade earlier. Tonti—known as "Iron Hand" because an iron hook replaced his left hand, which had been blown off by a grenade in a European conflict—was a lieutenant of the famous explorer René-Robert Cavalier, Sieur de La Salle, and accompanied him on his 1682 expedition into the lower Mississippi valley. He established the Arkansas Post, a trading post for the Quapaws, at the mouth of the Arkansas River in 1686. Three years after La Salle was murdered while traversing inland from the Texas coast in 1687, Tonti journeyed west from the Mississippi valley to search for survivors of La Salle's Texas colony. After returning to France, one of those survivors, Henri Joutel, wrote a journal of his adventures that he provided to Iberville (who apparently later returned it with pages missing).[3]

On his journey west from the Arkansas Post, Tonti brought two Kadohadacho women who had been captured and ransomed by the Osages. Along with Taensa guides, the French and Caddos crossed northern Louisiana and visited the Natchitoches. Natchitoches guides then escorted Tonti north to the Yatasi village. The Yatasis were in conflict with the Kadohadachos and refused to guide him farther, but they allowed the expedition to proceed upstream, where the travelers arrived at a Kadohadacho village on March 28, 1690. The captive women were reunited with a grateful and friendly Caddo people. Tonti was told that Frenchmen were living to the south at the Nabedache village—probably located on the upper Sabine River near the present Texas-Louisiana border. However, when the expedition arrived there, they found that Spanish troops had visited earlier, provided gifts, and warned the Caddos about Frenchmen with bad intentions. The Nabedache told Tonti that the Frenchmen formerly living there had left, but Tonti thought it likely that they had been killed, and he left the village on poor terms and returned to the Mississippi.

Spanish relationships with the Caddos did not turn out well either. After also looking for French survivors of the La Salle expedition, the Spanish installed missionaries at several Hasinai Caddo villages in 1690. In 1691 the Terán expedition crossed eastern Texas to the Kadohadachos, where an amazingly detailed (and now frequently studied) map of a Nasoni Caddo village was made (see chapter 5). However, over the course of the next couple of years, epidemics, crop failures, and resistance of the Caddos to religious conversion strained relations with missionaries and Spanish soldiers, and the missions were abandoned in 1693.

Caddos in the Eighteenth Century

Based on early chronicles, ethnologists and historians have argued that the Caddos were organized into three extensive "confederacies," the Kadohadacho, Hasinai, and Natchitoches, each composed of multiple "tribes" (fig. 53). It is not clear, however, how the confederacies were unified in political or social respects, or whether they had any formal associations at all. Early European visitors provided labels for specific communities at particular times, but connections between

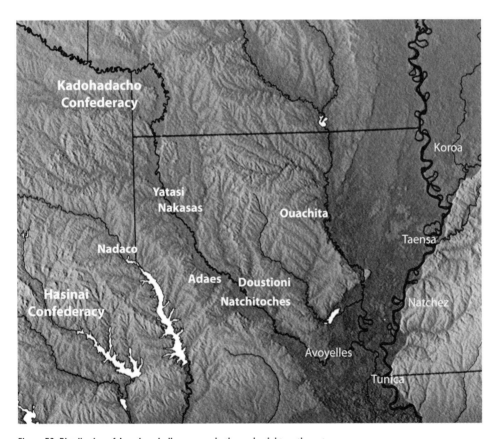

Figure 53. Distribution of American Indian groups in the early eighteenth century

communities were poorly understood by the colonists. It is apparent that some tribes, even those within the confederacies, at times were in conflict with one another and probably did not maintain formal, institutionalized political alliances. Confederacies might simply have been groups that lived in relatively close spatial proximity to one another with frequent social and economic interactions.[4]

In 1690, the Kadohadachos consisted of at least five tribes or extended communities located in Texas and Arkansas, both upstream and downstream from the Great Bend in the Red River. Only three of these remained in 1719. Derived from "Kadohadacho" is the name "Caddo," which eventually came to designate peoples in the Hasinai and Natchitoches confederacies as well.[5] Although several archaeological sites that date to the seventeenth and very early eighteenth centuries have been investigated in the Great Bend area, few historic documents relate to the Kadohadacho. Spanish missionaries recorded much information about the Hasinai groups in the Neches-Angelina River valleys of east-central Texas for the eighteenth century, and French records provide some information about the Natchitoches groups. French traders lived among the Kadohadachos, but they rarely wrote about their lives or described their trading partners. Available information indicates the likelihood that the Kadohadachos were very prosperous, engaged actively in trade with their southeastern and southern Plains neighbors, and were well respected militarily. Mounds, similar to the one at the Belcher site, probably continued to be used into the late seventeenth century, but there are no descriptions of mound construction or use after that time, possibly signifying some changes in Caddo ritual practices.

In what is now Louisiana, the Yatasis and Nakasas, the two groups encountered by the Bienville expedition, lived farthest to the northwest near the present-day Shreveport–Bossier City area. The Nakasa name shows up on a few early eighteenth-century maps, but the group appears to have either combined with the Yatasis or dispersed by midcentury. The Yatasis split into two groups around 1717 due to raids by the Chickasaws, a group from east of the Mississippi River who came west to acquire slaves. One Yatasi contingent went north to join the Kadohadacho confederacy, while the remainder moved south near the Natchitoches. The latter group apparently filtered back into the hills of what is now DeSoto Parish by the mid-eighteenth century and became important trading partners to the French.

The Natchitoches "confederacy" actually consisted of only two groups—the Natchitoches proper and the Doustioni, both of whom we first encountered in the Bienville narrative. The Natchitoches lived in a dispersed village along the Red River (now the channel known as Cane River); the Doustioni apparently set-

FIGURE 54. *The Founding of Natchitoches, 1714: St. Denis Trades with the Caddo Nation,* by H. B. Wright (*Courtesy of the Louisiana State Exhibit Museum, Shreveport*)

tled to the east along the Rigolet de Bon Dieu (now the main Red River channel), and perhaps a short distance upstream along Saline Bayou in Winn Parish.[6] One Frenchman on the Bienville expedition, Louis Juchereau de St. Denis, made several later trips up the Red River, and, in 1702, the Natchitoches, following a massive crop failure, accompanied him back south to the shore of Lake Pontchartrain to live alongside the Acolapissa Indians. The Doustioni apparently remained behind. Eleven years later, the Natchitoches returned to their old homeland with St. Denis and a handful of Frenchmen who established a trading post and Fort St. Jean Baptiste (fig. 54). The fate of the Doustioni is unknown; they disappear from the historic record during the eighteenth century.

Caddo culture remained dominant in northwest Louisiana into the mid-eighteenth century. A small French population settled around Fort St. Jean Baptiste and began the town of Natchitoches. The Natchitoches Caddos continued to reside in their dispersed village downstream from the fort until the late eighteenth century. Both the French and the Caddos grew foodstuffs, particularly corn and beans (and occasionally rice) for local consumption, but periodically shipped surpluses to New Orleans in exchange for European goods. They also cultivated peaches, plums, and grapes, and raised cows, chickens, pigs, turkeys, sheep, and goats. Tobacco farming began as early as the 1720s, but production was on a relatively small scale for local use. Significant commercial production began in the 1740s but did not become truly profitable until the Spanish period in the late 1760s. A few French farmers also produced indigo, a more arduous endeavor that necessitated considerable equipment and labor, both of which were in short supply.

The French settlement at Natchitoches was initially a trading post, and trade with American Indians continued to be of major importance throughout the early eighteenth century. Although most of the settlers remained in close spatial proximity to the fort while Louisiana was a French colony, a vigorous trade network developed between the French and the various Caddo groups. The French acquired goods such as hides, livestock, and bear oil in exchange for clothing, iron tools and vessels, weaponry, and other European-derived items. Located on the western frontier of the French holdings, Natchitoches became a node in an exchange complex that extended to New Orleans (established in 1717, a few years after the post at Natchitoches), and from there via large ships to the Caribbean and eventually Europe. Long-distance connections were increasing, and these would have profound effects on the peoples of northwest Louisiana.

The Natchitoches Cemeteries

Early twentieth-century archaeologists were enthusiastic about classifying material remains according to the "tribal" units identified in historical narratives, and thus sites that could be attributed to specific groups in historic time periods (particularly the eighteenth century) were eagerly sought. In 1931, Winslow Walker, an archaeologist from the Bureau of American Ethnology, conducted a survey along the Red River in an attempt to locate historic Coushatta and Natchitoches Indian sites. Walker was unable to locate Coushatta sites; however, he noted:

> In regard to Caddo sites we have been more fortunate. A year ago last summer an Indian burial ground was accidentally discovered near Natchitoches, which yielded elaborately engraved and incised, highly polished pottery associated with European trade objects such as glass beads and articles of brass and iron. This discovery I have made the subject of a brief report now awaiting publication. Its significance lies in the fact that we have been able to identify this site as the probable one occupied by the Natchitoches Indian village visited by Henri de Tonti in 1690 where he stated that he found the Natchitoches, Ouasita and Capiche tribes living together.[7]

In 1916, George Williamson of the Louisiana State Normal School (which later became Northwestern State University) excavated two burials, at least one of which included a Caddo bowl, in an area downstream from the town of Natchitoches. The area later was chosen for construction of the Natchitoches National Fish Hatchery, and in 1931 at least one hundred burials were reportedly uncovered by workmen (figs. 55 and 56). Walker interviewed W. A. Casler, the construction superintendent:

> He says they were all shallow interments, none deeper than 3 feet below the original ground surface, and all lying extended on their backs. Near the heads of many were pottery vessels in the form of bowls and pots, both decorated and plain, and in some cases glass and shell beads and metal objects as well. Mr. Casler noticed that many of the skeletons had curiously flattened skulls. Most surprising of all was the finding of two horse skeletons, each with a large earthen bowl placed near the head. The bowls were of plain ware about a foot and a half in diameter and half an inch thick. Very few stone or flint artifacts were found with any of the burials.[8]

Based on the workers' reports, Walker made a sketch map of the cemetery and was able to find and excavate one additional burial that had not been disturbed by the construction. The individual buried in this grave also exhibited flattening of the back of the skull, what is now called occipital cranial modeling, probably due to the practice of strapping infants onto cradle boards. Whether the reshap-

FIGURE 55. Looking west at the Natchitoches National Fish Hatchery (*Photo by Tommy Ike Hailey, Northwestern State University of Louisiana*)

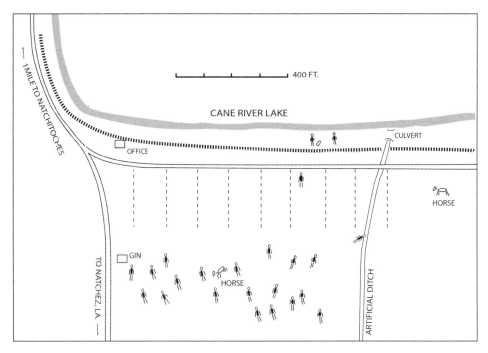

FIGURE 56. Winslow Walker's map of the historic Caddo cemetery at the Natchitoches National Fish Hatchery. (The north arrow has been left out as it was incorrect on the original map.) (*Modified from Walker 1935*)

ing of the skull was deliberate or an accidental result of the custom is not known. Although notable in the burials, the effects of cranial modeling on living individuals must have been subtle as European writers did not comment on unusual head shapes among the Caddos.

Gun parts and glass beads from the Fish Hatchery site appear to date very early in the eighteenth century. The Natchitoches clearly had horses and occasionally copied European pottery vessel forms. The large number of reported burials might indicate that the cemetery was used over a long span of time, with the latest interments perhaps relating to the early years after the French established the post at Fort St. Jean Baptiste. The presence of chipped stone and the lack of European trade goods (but similar pottery) at another Caddo cemetery found near Lawton Gin a few miles downstream might indicate that the Natchitoches village consisted of a dispersed community with multiple habitation and cemetery areas dating back at least as far as the late seventeenth century.

No residential areas contemporary with these cemeteries have been identified. An attempt to do so was made in 2001, when we decided to explore a dark soil layer that was buried a little over 1 m (3 ft) below the surface on the eastern side of the Fish Hatchery.[9] We excavated a large block of twelve 1 × 1 m (3 × 3 ft) squares and several peripheral units and found abundant broken pottery, stone tools, and animal bone, but no postholes or other evidence of architecture. Designs on the recovered pottery surprised us—they looked nothing like those on pottery found in the cemetery. We recovered several samples of charcoal for radiocarbon dating and found that the buried site dated to the fifteenth century, at least two hundred years before the burials reported by Walker. The pottery exhibited similarities to pottery found to the east in the Catahoula Basin region as well as to Caddo pottery to the north, raising the question as to whether the early inhabitants were a Caddo group directly ancestral to the historic Natchitoches or, alternatively, a culturally different people who had abandoned the area by the late seventeenth century.

Los Adaes: The Spanish Capital of Texas

European political events spilled over into the Americas by the early eighteenth century, sometimes in odd ways. In 1715, after the death of Louis XIV, the famous "Sun King," a crisis regarding the succession to the French throne developed. King Philip V of Spain was Louis's only surviving grandchild, but he was prevented from becoming the French king by the Treaty of Utrecht, which ended the War of the Spanish Succession (1701–13). Spain lost territories through this treaty and was eager to reacquire them. Philip claimed both the French and Spanish thrones, a move that greatly alarmed not only France but also other European nations such as England, Austria, and the Dutch Republic. War broke out between Spain and the allies in December 1718 (called the War of the Quadruple Alliance). In the Americas, French forces attacked Pensacola in May 1719 and eventually burned the Spanish presidio. On the western frontier in 1719, Lieutenant Philippe Blondel, commander of the French soldiers at Fort St. Jean Baptiste, decided to capture the Mission San Miguel de Linares de Los Adaes, which had been established by Spain twenty miles west of Natchitoches in 1716. Only one Spanish soldier and a lay brother were present at the time, and the latter managed to escape. The soldier was captured and taken to Fort St. Jean along with the mission's supply of chickens. Following what became known as the "Chicken War," Spain made efforts to reestablish its presence in the area. The conflict between France and Spain ended in 1720, and the following year the Spanish constructed a new mission, Mission San Miguel de Cuellar de Los Adaes, and a presidio, Nuestra Señora del Pilár de Los Adaes, a few miles from the previous location. Los Adaes was designated the capital of the province of Texas. The presidio was initially populated by one hundred soldiers, but because of the distance from other Spanish facilities and the close relationship of the American Indians to the French, Los Adaes proved difficult to supply and became reliant on (illegal) trade with the French at Natchitoches. Nevertheless, the mission and presidio remained in operation until 1772, a few years after the 1767 cession of Louisiana to Spain.

The Adaes were a tribe whose relationship with the Natchitoches and other Caddo groups is not well understood. In a manuscript written about 1718, Bienville claimed that they lived around the mission and numbered about one hundred men. A French trader, Bernard de la Harpe, traveled up the Red River in 1719 to establish a trading post among the Kadohadachos. On his way, he passed through two "Yatay" (Adaes) villages and noted that they lived on the river only when the water was low. On his return trip later in the year, la Harpe fell ill and was treated by Adaes "sorcerers." A total population of about four hundred Adaes was noted by Father Morfi in 1721. Many years later, Indian agent John Sibley noted that the Adaes had a divergent and difficult language but also spoke Caddo and French.[10]

Hiram F. "Pete" Gregory of Northwestern State University initiated archaeological research at Los Adaes in 1965.[11] Concentrating on the presidio, Gregory carried out several projects into the mid-1980s that resulted in the detection of portions of the palisade trench and bastions, possible kitchen and blacksmith areas, and the governor's house. Interpretations were aided by the survival of an architect's plan made prior to the presidio construction, and by a map made by Joseph Urrutia in 1767 that depicted conditions in amazing detail as they existed shortly before abandonment (fig. 57). The map includes the locations of several small outlying structures situated on the periphery of the presidio (about forty houses were reported by a French visitor in 1768). Gregory's excavations identified three small structures including a house that probably was occupied by a French trader after the presidio had been abandoned.

The Louisiana Division of Archaeology sponsored George Avery as station archaeologist at the site in 1995, and he synthesized previous work, conducted additional analyses on recovered artifacts, and carried out excavations in areas damaged by fallen trees (fig. 58). Avery also supervised excavations carried out to verify information that was acquired during a project using archaeogeophysical technologies, which are of increasing importance in archaeological research. These technologies involve use of instruments that are able to detect "anomalies" or features beneath the surface that differ from the surrounding undisturbed sediments.

Geophysical technology consists of both active and passive techniques. Active

FIGURE 57. Artistic reconstruction of Los Adaes presidio by Sergio Palleroni, based on the 1767 map by Joseph Ur-rutia (*Courtesy of the Louisiana Department of Culture, Recreation and Tourism, Division of Archaeology*)

FIGURE 58. Aerial view of the Los Adaes presidio (*Photo by Tommy Ike Hailey, Northwestern State University of Louisiana*)

techniques transmit electromagnetic energy into the ground and measure the response to subsurface characteristics. Passive technologies measure inherent or naturally occurring and culturally altered physical properties without introducing additional electrical or magnetic energy. Probably the most frequently used (and most successful) technique is known as gradiometry (a form of magnetometry). It is a passive technology that measures small variations in the earth's natural magnetic alignment that result from sediments having been disturbed. Sediments subjected to intense burning also have a distinctly different magnetic signature than their surroundings. Gradiometry is highly sensitive to the presence of iron artifacts, which can be a problem in areas where recently discarded metal items or wire fences are present. The gradiometer is a hand-held instrument that is passed across the surface in linear alignments. Electrical resistance, an active technology, involves passing an electrical current between two probes and measuring variation in the voltage. Prospection depth is controlled by the distance of separation between the probes (fig. 59). This technology depends on differences in physical properties of the soil such as moisture, dissolved ions, and soil particle size. The physical properties of archaeological features commonly differ from the surrounding natural soil matrix, resulting in measurable differential resistance to the flow of electricity. For example, the moist fill of a buried ditch might provide a less resistant pathway for electrical current than the surrounding dry and compacted natural soil matrix.

FIGURE 59. Scanning the surface of the Los Adaes mission site using electrical resistivity.

In 2009, a project was carried out at the presidio by the U.S. Army Engineer Research and Development Center (ERDC) Construction Engineering Research Laboratory (CERL) and the Center for Advanced Spatial Technologies (CAST), University of Arkansas. A later project was conducted in the mission area. The results of the archaeogeophysics at the presidio were superb (fig. 60). Magnetic and resistivity picked up linear alignments that subsequent test excavations veri-

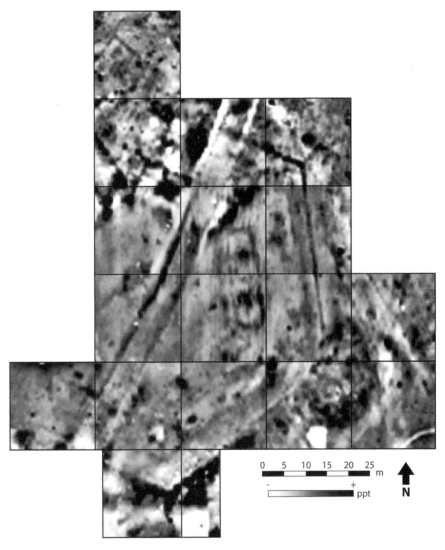

FIGURE 60. Magnetic susceptibility data for the western portion of the Los Adaes presidio. The bastion, palisade wall trench, and interior structures are clearly visible. The wide stripe through the center of the presidio is an early twentieth-century road. [*Image produced as part of the project "Streamlined Archaeo-Geophysical Data Processing and Integration for DoD Field Use," funded by the Environmental Security Technology Certification Program, ESTCP Project No. 200611; courtesy of Eileen Ernenwein*]

fied represented the palisade wall trench. Also identified were concentrations of trash that had been used by the soldiers to build up an earthen platform on which to place cannon in the southwest bastion. A possible hearth or earth oven within one of the structures in the presidio also produced a large anomaly. Excavations conducted in 2010 confirmed the existence of most of the features detected by the geophysics.

The Spanish soldiers and clergy at Los Adaes lived among American Indians and the nearby French at Natchitoches in peaceful terms during the mid-eighteenth century, despite official Spanish restrictions on trade that was vital to all the groups. Although the mission to convert the Adaes to Christianity was a failure, the presidio prevented the French from expanding to the west and helped maintain peaceful relations with the American Indians. Excavations at Los Adaes have provided the best record of eighteenth-century material culture for northwest Louisiana (fig. 61). Caddo, French, and Spanish pottery are all well represented, with Caddo pottery by far the most numerous. The structures within the presidio appear to have been constructed similar to traditional French practices, but small buildings on the periphery exhibit traits of both Spanish *jacales* and traditional Caddo houses.

The French and the Spanish adopted many of the practices of their Caddo neighbors regarding use of the landscape and food production. However, although numerically superior to French and Spanish colonists and maintaining political control of northwest Louisiana into the mid-eighteenth century, the Caddos became increasingly dependent on French material culture. By midcentury, the Caddos were clothed in French cloth, used metal tools, rode horses for overland transportation, relied on guns, lead shot, and powder for hunting as well as defense (although the bow and arrow continued to be used into the early nineteenth century), and began to consume significant quantities of alcohol. To acquire these goods, the Caddos provided bison and deer hides, bear fat, and livestock (obtained primarily from Comanche and Wichita groups in Texas, who procured them from raids of Spanish ranches) to French traders. They also sold war captives, particularly Apaches, as slaves. The trade flourished even as disease slowly depleted the Caddo population, and the number of constituent groups for each of the confederacies declined as groups consolidated or disappeared. The spatial proximity and economic ties between American Indians, the Spanish, and the French produced an increasingly complex social environment where formerly distinct traditional lifeways merged, and even ethnic identities blended, as we explore in chapter 7.

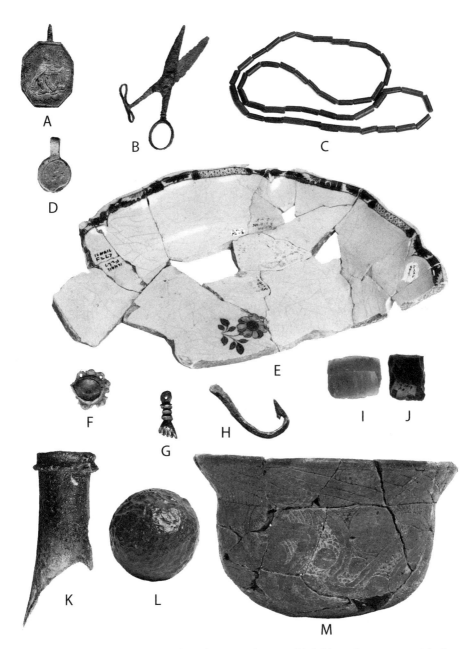

FIGURE 61. The excavations at Los Adaes have given us a unique sample of eighteenth-century material culture. Among the artifacts recovered from presidio Nuestra Señora del Pilár de Los Adaes are a religious medal (A); scissors (B); glass beads (C); a lead cloth seal (D); a Spanish majolica plate (E); an earring (F); a silver amulet (G); a fishing hook (H); French and English gunflints (I–J); a wine bottle fragment (K); a cannonball (L); and a Caddo-made engraved ceramic bowl (M). (*Photos by Don Sepulvado, Northwestern State University of Louisiana*)

7

TRANSITIONS TO MODERNITY
(CA. AD 1760–1835)

On September 10, 1805, Francis Roban and Joseph Lucas, two young men working for the traders Oliver and Case, were transporting horses and deer hides from the Kadohadacho village near Caddo Lake south to Natchitoches. They stopped for the night at the home of Athanase Poissot, a resident of Bayou Pierre, a dispersed multiethnic community that encompassed a broad geographic region along the eastern edge of the hills overlooking the Red River floodplain stretching from what is now northern Natchitoches Parish to the Wallace Lake area between DeSoto and Caddo Parishes. The following morning Roban went to the nearby house of Manuel DeSoto, a syndic, or local official for the Spanish government. Although the political situation was murky, Spain considered the Bayou Pierre settlement as lying within its jurisdiction despite the recent Louisiana Purchase by the United States. Roban was captured by several Spanish soldiers who insisted that he take them to alleged smugglers Oliver and Case. Roban led the soldiers about eight miles south to the house of Pierre Dolet, but when they did not find the traders, Roban's hands were tied with a rope and the group returned to Poissot's place. By then, Roban's friend Lucas had left with the horses and hides. The Spaniards, with their captive in tow, were able to follow tracks to the home of Pierre Robleau, located along Bayou Nabonchasse on the northern periphery of the Bayou Pierre community.

It was about eight o'clock on a moonlit night. The soldiers found the smuggled horses grazing on the Robleau property. They drove them into a horse pen, untied Roban, and placed him under guard in the pen. The Spanish corporal then packed a couple of pistols and set off to capture Lucas, whose campfire was visible in the distance. About fifteen minutes later, the corporal came running back out of breath and exclaimed, "Blast the Indian, he wanted to shoot me with his arrow." A Yatasi Indian immediately followed, and the Spaniard raised his pistol. The Indian told him, "You had best be easy, for I am not a child; you may thank me that you are here now." The corporal calmed down and apologized. Later that night the Indian crept back into the horse pen and told Roban that he would help him overcome and tie the Spaniards, or else kill them if he preferred. Roban did not agree to this, and the next morning the Spaniards, along with Roban and the horses, started back south to the DeSoto place. As they passed Robleau's house, Roban asked to stop for a drink of water. Once in the house, he escaped out the back door and hid in a cotton field, then spent the night in a nearby thicket. The soldiers left with the smuggled goods and Roban's horse, saddle, and bridle. Roban returned to the house, where Robleau fed him and warned that he should avoid the main road as the Spaniards were determined to recapture him. Roban eventually made it back to Natchitoches and provided a deposition of the events to Justice of the Peace John Sibley.[1]

Roban's narrative provides fascinating details of the local social, economic, and political situation in northwest Louisiana during the early nineteenth century. Following the defeat of France in the Seven Years' War (or French and Indian War, as it is called in America), the French territory of Louisiana had been transferred to Spain in 1762. This Louisiana Cession gave rise to profound changes in economic and settlement configurations in what now constitutes the northwestern quarter of the state of Louisiana. Spanish economic policies and precipitous declines in American Indian populations resulted in a transformed social landscape by the time of the 1803 Louisiana Purchase. Because the eastern border was too extensive to control by available military means, the Spanish government tried to stimulate capital and labor by increasing population. Immigration laws were liberalized in 1788, and the Crown provided generous land grants, encouraged importation of African slaves, and became more tolerant of Protestantism. Despite a 1768 royal decree broadening trade privileges of the colonists, Spain attempted to retain tight control over commerce in Louisiana. Working against the desired economic effect, however, were English smugglers traveling down the Mississippi River offering English goods at lower cost and of better quality. New Orleans was eventually opened to limited commerce with Anglo-American traders on the Mississippi River, but this strategy failed to make Louisiana profitable to Spain, and loyalty to the Spanish Crown was tepid or absent throughout most of the colony. Spain secretly returned Louisiana to France in 1800, who then sold it to the United States in 1803. However, the western boundary between Louisiana and Texas, which remained within the confines of New Spain, was a matter of contention until the Sabine River was agreed upon through the Adams-Onís Treaty of 1819 (ratified in 1821).

The Bayou Pierre Settlement

During the Spanish period, population dispersal from the immediate Natchitoches area occurred in two directions.[2] Downstream in the Red River floodplain to the south of Natchitoches, the Bayou Brevelle and Rivière aux Cannes communities commenced with Spanish land grants to farmers who grew cash crops such as tobacco and indigo, and who engaged in subsistence farming and small-scale ranching. The hilly uplands to the west and northwest became the home of dispersed settlers constituting the community generally referred to as Bayou Pierre. In economic terms, the Bayou Pierre settlement was based on ranching, small-scale subsistence farming, and the continuance of trade with the Caddos as well as with Wichita and Comanche groups (collectively known as the Norteños) who had recently moved into the prairies of north Texas.

Trade between French colonists and nearby American Indian groups was ongoing from the start of the Natchitoches settlement. A trading post known as La Pointe, established as early as the 1730s, was accessible by water from Natchitoches along a western route circumventing the Great Raft (the exact location of La Pointe is unknown, but it probably was near Smithport Lake in DeSoto Parish). The Indian trade continued into the Spanish period. Sometime in the mid-1770s, following abandonment of the presidio and mission at Los Adaes, families from Natchitoches, including a few Hispanic refugees from the Adaes community who had refused to evacuate to San Antonio in 1773, started moving into the hill country above the Spanish Lake lowlands and along Bayou Pierre, where they established farms and ranches amid the remnants of the Yatasi, Adaes, and Natchitoches Indians, whose numbers were in decline. The Bayou Pierre settlement took its name from the Bayou aux Pierres—Bayuco de las Piedras in Spanish—a small upland drainage near present-day Naborton that corresponds to the stream now known as Sawmill Creek and Mundy Bayou. The name, which translates as "stony creek," refers to the stream's clear running waters, gravelly bed, and nearby bedrock outcrops.

Some of this new territory was considered uninhabited by the Spanish government and was simply granted to colonists. Other areas were recognized as Caddo (primarily Yatasi) territory and were purchased by Natchitoches residents. Pierre Dolet established a ranch in 1761, and others arrived in the late 1770s. Approximately thirty families were present by the time of the Louisiana Purchase. Although most of the settlers were of French or Spanish descent, American Indians including Lipan Apache slaves or concubines, African ranch hands, and peoples of English, Irish, and German heritage also were present. Bayou Pierre settlers exported cereal grains and livestock to both Natchitoches and Nacogdoches. Attempts apparently were made to grow tobacco during the Spanish period, but output was minimal compared to that from the Red River. In 1804 John Sibley noted that the district contained large herds of cattle and produced excellent cheese and ham. Corn, tobacco, and cotton were the staple crops, along with production of garden vegetables and cultivated fruits for domestic consumption. Although the exchange of livestock, guns, and deerskins, which had begun in French colonial times, expanded during the last decades of the eighteenth century, the American Indian population declined precipitously. In addition to traders such as Paul Bouet Laffitte, Bernard D'Ortolant, and Marcel DeSoto who were able to procure passports to trade with the Indians legally, many Bayou Pierre settlers engaged in freelance trading. Little attention was paid to the laws prohibiting trade with Texas, and the inhabitants of the district were continually accused of engaging in illegal commerce. Most of the contraband trade between Louisiana and Texas passed through Bayou Pierre between roughly 1770 and 1810, and commerce between Natchitoches Post and the Kadohadacho villages proceeded by boat through passages around the Great Raft or by horse and wagon along the upland divide between the Red and Sabine Rivers.

Because many of the early Bayou Pierre settlers remained in the area after the Louisiana Purchase, the locations of their households appear on some of the land survey plats that date to the 1830s, and a few places have been subject to archaeological investigation including the homeplace of Pierre Robleau where Francis Roban escaped the Spanish soldiers. Robleau was born in Natchitoches in 1769, and, in 1800, he married and set up a new household at the northern edge of the Bayou Pierre community along a small stream known as Bayou Nabonchasse.[3] Pierre was the son of a soldier at Fort St. Jean Baptiste in Natchitoches, his mother was of Spanish descent, and his wife, Magdeleine, was the "natural" daughter of Bastien Prudhomme and Naillois, who is listed as a *métis* or *sauvagesse* (perhaps Caddo) in the French records. The Robleaus had at least five children. The eldest daughter, Marie Susette, married Philip Flores (whose father had been a soldier at Los Adaes) in 1818, at which time they apparently set up a separate household on the adjoining property. After coming of age, son Pierre Jr. also may have constructed a house on his father's land. Three other children, two sons and a daughter, are listed in baptismal records. A servant (perhaps field hand), Juan Malrone, noted to be of Irish descent, is identified in an 1805 Spanish census. Later the Robleaus had an African slave named Susanne, who baptized at least three children. Pierre Robleau was listed on the 1840 census but apparently died shortly thereafter.

Archaeological remains relating to the early nineteenth century were uncovered on the lower slopes of a series of ridges along Bayou Nabonchasse after timber was cut in the fall of 2001. I was notified of the sites by Judson Rives of Mansfield, who has identified many archaeological sites in the region. The landowner allowed us to examine the area before it was replanted in pine. The most extensive scatter of artifacts was on the eastern ridge, where we identified a shallow pit, probably directly beneath the location of the former Robleau house, as well as an area of ash and burned clay that likely represents the fireplace and collapsed chimney. It is not clear whether the house was a log, plank, or bousillâge structure. Small brick fragments and many nails were present but not concentrated in the hearth area. An abundant and diverse collection of artifacts was recovered; almost all appear to date between approximately 1790 and 1840.

As at many archaeological sites, the most numerous artifacts were potsherds (fig. 62). Imported English pottery was by far the most common—undecorated creamware and pearlware with shell-edged, hand-painted floral, annular, and transfer-printed decorations. Only a small amount of French faience was present. French pottery rapidly dropped out of use in the late eighteenth century with the increasing availability of less expensive and better-quality English ceramics. Thick, hard stoneware pottery, used primarily for storage vessels (crockery), was scarce. Almost a quarter of the total sherds came from locally made vessels tempered with crushed mussel shell. This pottery—often referred to as "colonoware"—likely was made by the Yatasis and other Caddo Indians and included

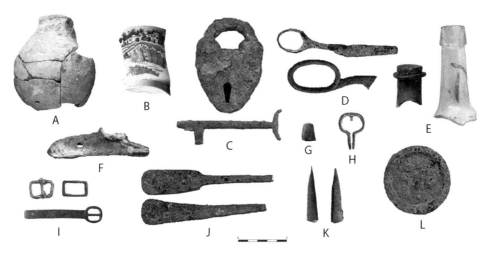

FIGURE 62. Artifacts from the Robleau site: colonoware pitcher (A); transfer-printed bowl fragment (B); iron lock and key (C); scissors (D); glass bottle fragments (E); gun side plate (F); brass thimble (G); mouth harp (H); iron and brass buckles (I); spoon or fork handles (J); copper cones (K); 1-pound iron scale weight (L)

brimmed bowls, pitchers (with handles), and deep bowls that mimic European vessels rather than match traditional American Indian forms. Nonceramic containers consisted primarily of glass bottle fragments. Cast-iron kettles were very popular in the late eighteenth and early nineteenth centuries, and several broken specimens were found at the Robleau sites.

A few iron tools and utensils were present, although most were in poor condition. Included were fork or spoon handles, scissors, a chisel, awls or picks, and knife fragments. A brass thimble also was found (Magdeleine Robleau identified herself as a seamstress in an 1804 Spanish census). Other interesting metal items include an iron padlock with a brass keyhole cover, as well as an iron key. Horse gear was confined to a few iron horse (or mule?) shoe fragments. Items connected with weaponry include a few gun parts (lock plates and a breech plug), stone gunflints (both English and French), and lead shot. A one-pound iron scale weight possibly was used to weigh shot or gunpowder, or other bulk items traded by Robleau including salt or locally grown grain and cotton. Two conical points of copper may have served to tip spears. Interestingly, several stone dart points of Archaic-period styles were recovered. It is not clear whether these represent a much earlier occupation of the area, or whether they were collected (and used?) by the Robleau family. Other stone items included several gunflints that originated in both England and France.

Cloth and leather do not preserve in the strongly acidic soils of the area, but several brass buttons, a bone button, and two small iron buckles were recovered. We also found several glass beads—a common artifact on contemporary sites, but often missed in surface collections because of their small size. The beads may have been sewn on clothing or accessories. Other important items for the Robleaus were kaolin smoking pipes; we came across numerous stem fragments.

Within the shallow pit that probably underlay the Robleau house we recovered animal bones and turtle shell. Wild species dominated—mostly deer, but also squirrel, rabbit, possum, raccoon, turkey, duck, and a couple of wolf bones. Shell fragments from box turtles were especially numerous. Turtle often is found on precolonial Caddo sites, and it is possible that Magdeleine Robleau favored use of turtle stemming from her American Indian heritage (although we know nothing about her upbringing). No plant remains were preserved, but a grinding stone possibly for processing maize was found. It is likely that the Robleaus collected hickory nuts and pecans, as well as persimmons, sunflowers, and various berries. They may have cultivated fruits such as peaches as well.

Like most families living in rural areas at that time, the Robleaus were not economically specialized. They made a living through a combination of subsistence farming or gardening, hunting, fishing, gathering wild plant foods, and raising livestock for domestic consumption, as well as by trading manufactured goods to the Caddos in exchange for products such as horses, cattle, deer hides, and bear oil. Most of the family's material goods had to be purchased—iron tools and utensils, weaponry, pottery, iron kettles, wine, textiles, and other items were acquired from Natchitoches merchants who obtained the goods from New Orleans. Overland transportation was extremely slow and difficult. Freight had to be moved with horses and saddlebags, or horses and wagons along the few existing roads passable during the drier seasons. Most goods probably were transported up the Red River in rafts, pirogues, and keelboats. Henry Shreve's boat *Enterprise* traveled from New Orleans to Natchitoches as early as 1815, and steamboat traffic extended to Coates' Bluff (now in southeast Shreveport) by the mid-1830s following early efforts at raft removal by Shreve. Steamboat travel could be extremely dangerous, however, as exploding boilers were an ongoing problem throughout the early nineteenth century. Challenges with transportation affected the movement not only of material goods but of information in general. The isolation of rural families is difficult to comprehend in our modern times of radio, television, cell phones, and the Internet. Electricity was known but had not been put to use in any practical ways. The telegraph was not available until the 1840s, and then only in limited areas. Thus, information was communicated by travelers and visitors, perhaps sometimes bringing newspapers or books.[4]

Thus, families in the Bayou Pierre community acquired basic household items and tools through surplus production that likely resulted primarily from profits gained through the Indian trade. Kinship may have been important in these transactions—perhaps Magdeleine's American Indian heritage provided important trading partners and might be one reason for Robleau's initial movement from Natchitoches to the fringes of the settlement. Labor was conducted primarily by the families themselves, although temporary field hands (including the Irishman Juan Malrone) may have been employed. This situation was very different from the farming operations that were beginning to develop in the Red River floodplain downstream from Natchitoches, where prosperity was linked to cash crops and necessitated enslaved labor. The Robleaus had only a single female slave, and it is likely she was engaged as a housekeeper.

When Robleau first set up his household, political conditions were highly unsettled. There was a need to balance local interests with the Spanish–United States border situation and to maintain cordial relations with the Yatasis and other American Indians. Robleau identified himself as a farmer probably because of the legal restrictions on trade prior to ratification of the Adams-Onís Treaty in

1821, officially making the region part of the United States. Robleau was of French heritage, born a citizen of Spain, married to a woman of partial American Indian heritage, and living under the United States government only during the last two decades of his life. Modern notions of patriotic connections to nation-states did not exist in colonial borderland situations such as this, and he likely had little loyalty to France, Spain, or the United States. At the time of Robleau's death in the early 1840s, political, social, and economic circumstances in northwest Louisiana were undergoing profound changes. Removal of major portions of the Red River raft led to the opening of steamboat traffic and availability of new lands for farming. There was an influx of Anglo-Americans from Mississippi, Alabama, Tennessee, Georgia, and other areas to the east, and many new settlers brought wealth and slaves, expanding the cotton economy. The original Bayou Pierre settlers became marginalized both socially and politically, but their descendants continue to reside in the region today.

Final Years of the Caddos in Louisiana

On June 25, 1835, almost five hundred Caddo Indians gathered at the agency house on Peach Orchard Bluff. Federal troops were there to keep outside agitators out, and they turned away Manuel Flores, Francis Bark, and Joseph Valentin, longtime friends of the Caddos and residents of the ethnically mixed Bayou Pierre community. The Caddos had come to formalize what had become a fait accompli, the sale of their homelands to the United States government. Since 1825 these lands had been officially delineated as lying between Bayou Pierre on the east, the border with Mexico on the west, the mouth of the Sulphur River on the north, and Cypress Bayou on the south. After an initial payment of thirty thousand dollars' worth of horses and goods, the Caddos were to receive ten thousand dollars in cash for each of the next five years. In return, they would leave and agree never to return. Although some Caddos remained for a time in northwest Louisiana, the Caddo Treaty of 1835 essentially ended an era of Caddo cultural ascendancy that had lasted more than one thousand years. Much of the legacy of this long history of the human past languished and was lost to the new inhabitants of the region. What had happened to change Caddo fortunes so dramatically in less than the span of a century?

Although considered a colony by France, most of Louisiana remained primarily an American Indian place until the middle of the eighteenth century. As noted above, during the Spanish period, settlements from the immediate Natchitoches area expanded in two general directions—the hilly uplands to the west and northwest, which became the home of the Bayou Pierre community; and the Red River floodplain to the south of Natchitoches, where the Bayou Brevelle and Rivière aux Cannes communities commenced with Spanish land grants to farmers.

Economic relations between the Caddos and Europeans changed substantially during the late eighteenth century. The earliest European goods acquired by the Caddos were nonutilitarian in nature. Early eighteenth-century gifts from French explorers were described as "trinkets" and included items such as glass beads and mirrors. These objects did not induce any fundamental changes in Caddo life but probably took on traditional meanings and importance similar to the copper and marine-shell luxury goods found in mortuary contexts in earlier times. Although European goods were acquired as part of a system of exchange as noted above, many were considered gifts that were essentially tribute paid by the colonists in return for security because they lacked the population and military power to defend themselves. The demographic situation shifted, however, and the Caddos became dependent on more practical goods obtained from European sources, including iron tools, weaponry, and clothing (fig. 63). Supplying trade items in return became increasingly difficult. An inventory of gifts given in 1770 to the Yatasis by Athanase de Mézières, the Spanish lieutenant governor at Natchitoches, includes clothing, guns, powder and shot, metal tools and containers, ornamental items, salt, tobacco, and liquor.[5]

As the number of colonists increased, differing concepts about ownership and use of the landscape became important. Purchases of Caddo lands from individual Caddos were noted in legal records, but the status of the sellers within Caddo society is not always clear. Were certain lands considered to be the property of individual Caddos and thus amenable to sale in the European sense? Did enterprising Caddos offer lands over which they actually had little or no control? Did land sellers act as spokespersons for their communities, and did the exchanged goods fall under the control of community leaders? What changes took place in Caddo society as a result of these transactions? The historic record, produced by outsiders to Caddo society, is largely silent on these issues. Traditional Caddo use of lands appears to have been open, with extensive tracts exploited for hunting, fishing, and gathering wild plant foods. Villages were moved when small-scale crop production was no longer viable on adjoining plots of land. This system conflicted with eighteenth-century European notions of private land ownership, considered by Enlightenment thinkers as among the "natural" rights of the individual.

The position of the Natchitoches Caddos became precarious as the desire for farmland increased in the former French colony. In 1764 and 1765, traditional

Cadós.

Cados ou Caddoquis : Indigènes des environs de Nacogdoches.

FIGURE 63. Caddo couple in Nacogdoches, Texas, in 1828, drawn by Lino Sánchez y Tapia after José María Sánchez y Tapia (*Bound Book of Watercolors, Cados, Plate 8, Gilcrease Museum, Tulsa*)

Caddo village lands were sold, and the community moved a few miles north of town—a 1766 Spanish census reported only ten Caddos living next to Fort St. Jean Baptiste.[6] Although population numbers for the various Caddo groups are very difficult to reconstruct, it has been estimated that the Natchitoches Caddos consisted of about 1,800 people in 1700 but already were suffering a rapid decline when the French colonists arrived. Only about 700 remained in 1720, and there were fewer than 500 by midcentury.[7] In 1778 the Trichel and Grappe families purchased lands from a Caddo named Tsaqua Camté (beginning the town now known as Campti), and the remaining Natchitoches moved fifteen to twenty miles upstream. Indian agent John Sibley reported that only twelve men and nineteen women remained in the Natchitoches tribe in 1805. Disease was a primary factor in the population decline. American Indians lacked immunity from European-introduced diseases such as influenza and smallpox, both of which likely were brought into the region as early as the 1540 De Soto expedition. Several epidemics occurred during the eighteenth century, with a 1778 smallpox outbreak being particularly devastating to the Caddos.

By the middle of the eighteenth century, the Yatasis had resettled within and on the edge of the emerging Bayou Pierre community in northern Natchitoches and DeSoto Parishes. They were intensively involved in the trade between Natchitoches and the American Indian groups (Kadohadacho and Norteño) to the north and west, and, as noted in the Roban narrative, they maintained close ties to the French even after the Spanish Cession. On several occasions, Yatasi leaders threatened to attack Spanish settlements and soldiers when Spain attempted to intervene in the Yatasi-French trade. The group may have been less dependent on agriculture than the Natchitoches and Kadohadachos and apparently moved frequently as game supplies and trade routes shifted. Researchers have not been able to locate an eighteenth-century Yatasi habitation site in the archaeological record, although it is possible that Yatasis were early occupants of the Robleau and nearby Louis Procello sites.

A 1766 Spanish census noted thirty Yatasi families. In 1805 Sibley reported: "Of the ancient Yatassees there are but eight men remaining, and twenty-five women, besides children; but a number of men of other nations have intermarried with them, and live together. I paid a visit to their village the last summer; there were about forty men of them altogether. Their original language differs from any other; but now, all speak Caddo. They live on rich land, raise plenty of corn, beans, pumpkins, tobacco, &c., have horses, cattle, hogs, and poultry."[8] Most of the Yatasis apparently joined with the Kadohadachos in signing the 1835 treaty. In 1790 the remaining Kadohadacho groups consolidated and ten years later moved south to a village known as Sha'chahdínnih, or Timber Hill, located along James Bayou near Caddo Lake. While there, the Caddos attempted to maintain the traditional farming, hunting, and fishing economy that they practiced in the Red River floodplain, but they were now situated on much poorer lands. During late autumn most of the men traveled west to the southern plains to hunt bison (mostly for trade). An archaeological site found in the late 1990s by Claude McCrocklin and members of the Louisiana and Texas archaeological societies is in the approximate area where the Caddo village was plotted on early nineteenth-century maps.[9] The site contains a mixture of Caddo and English pottery similar to that at the Robleau site. Other artifacts also are very similar; in fact, if it were not for the historic records, it is unlikely that it would be possible to identify the inhabitants showing how pervasive imported, mass-produced (primarily English) material goods had become in the early nineteenth century.

Diminishment of game supplies, drought, flooding, disease, and other factors caused economic conditions to deteriorate despite the efforts of men such as Tinhiouen and Dehahuit, both incredibly astute and passionate leaders who held the diverse Caddo peoples together and maintained relations with Spain and the new government of the United States. Dehahuit died in 1833 as Henry Shreve was clearing the Great Raft near what would shortly become the city of Shreveport. A rapid influx of settlers from the east occurred, settlers eager to acquire the best farmlands within the remaining Caddo territory. After signing the treaty in 1835, most of the remaining Caddos, now including the Hasinais, moved westward to Texas, but shortly thereafter they were displaced again, this time into Indian Territory, where they settled in 1859. The Caddo Nation survived, and its members now number about five thousand, maintaining a tribal government near Binger, Oklahoma. There they carry on many traditions, including social dances such as the Turkey Dance, which commemorates their history and the accomplishments of Caddo warriors. Several families of the Adaes remained in their traditional homeland near Spanish Lake, north of the old presidio and mission. Their descendants continue to reside in the area and are a state-recognized tribe.

Caddo culture is a fundamental component of the heritage of the state of Louisiana. It is truly unfortunate that the legacy of the Caddo people, a legacy that comprises the major portion of the human past in the northwest portion of the state, is so poorly known and rarely appreciated and celebrated. Most of the Caddo past is accessible only through studies of the archaeological record. This record is very fragile and continues to be degraded by modern alterations to the landscape and by the pernicious activities of relic hunters seeking personal souvenirs. It is my hope that this book will contribute to a new awareness of the deep and dynamic past of the earliest residents of Louisiana and of the immense importance of respecting, carefully researching, and preserving the vestiges of the lifeways of our predecessors.

NOTES

1. Archaeology and Human History in Northwest Louisiana

1. The Louisiana Division of Archaeology, Department of Culture, Recreation and Tourism provides an excellent set of teaching materials and interactive exhibits (www.crt.state.la.us/ ARCHAEOLOGY/). See also the Tejas (Caddo) Exhibit in the Texas Beyond History website (www .texasbeyondhistory.net/tejas/index.html).

2. Wolf 1982.

2. The Earliest Peoples of Northwest Louisiana (ca. 11,500–500 BC)

1. I recommend an excellent summary by Meltzer 2009.

2. Dr. Clarence Hungerford Webb (1902–1991) was a Shreveport pediatrician who was also a pioneer of archaeological research in Louisiana.

3. For those interested in kinship systems of the Caddos, see Lesser and Weltfish 1932; Parsons 1941; and Swanton 1942.

4. This section is derived from Girard et al. 2011.

5. Jackson and Scott 2001.

6. Peacock 2008.

7. B. Smith 1986.

3. The Woodland Period and Early Mounds in Northwest Louisiana (ca. 500 BC–AD 900)

1. Beyer 1897.

2. The discovery and careful documentation of these early mounds by Joe Saunders of the University of Louisiana at Monroe (and northeast regional archaeologist for the Louisiana Division of Archaeology) has been one of the most exciting and important advances for Louisiana archaeology in modern times (see Saunders et al. 2005).

3. Although Poverty Point has been extensively researched and written about, only a small fraction of the site has been investigated, and there is much to learn. Excellent overviews include Ford and Webb 1956; Webb 1982; Gibson 2000; Ellerbe and Greenlee 2015; and the nomination document for the World Heritage List (Greenlee 2013).

4. For information on the Marksville site and associated times, see McGimsey 2010.

5. This section is derived from Girard 2012.

6. See Fulton and Webb 1953; Webb 1984; and Girard 2012. The following discussion is taken largely from Girard 2012.

7. The reader will see that considerable effort went into the excavation of human burials in the early to mid-twentieth century. Today, increased sensitivity to the concerns of modern American Indians has changed our practices, and burials are no longer excavated without consultation with descendant groups. In Louisiana, it is against the law to disturb a human burial regardless of the age. An Unmarked Burial Board that includes American Indian members is authorized to issue permits when circumstances necessitate exhumation and reburial.

8. McClurkan, Field, and Woodall 1966; Jensen 1968.

9. Walker 1936.

10. Lee 2010; Lee et al. 2011.

11. Girard 2000.

4. Beginnings of Caddo Culture (ca. AD 900–1300)

1. Mooney 1896.

2. Many books and articles about Cahokia are available. I recommend Pauketat 2009 as a current and insightful summary.

3. Weinstein, Kelley, and Saunders 2003.

5. Organization of the Caddos in Precolonial Times (ca. AD 1300–1700)

1. Girard 2012.

2. Unfortunately, there is no scale on the map, but it is estimated that the village may have extended as far as 9 km (5.6 mi) in length.

3. Eighteenth-century Caddo social organization is discussed in Swanton 1942 and Bolton 1987.

4. Webb 1983.

5. Swanton 1942:228.

6. Webb 1959.

6. Caddos and Colonials (ca. AD 1700–1760)

1. The description and the quotations from Bienville's journey are from McWilliams 1981.

2. Some reconstructions indicate that the 1540–41 De Soto expedition crossed northwest Louisiana. Recent studies suggest a more northerly route (see Girard, Perttula, and Trubitt 2014).

3. Joutel's journal survived in two versions: a 1715 account that was translated to English (Joutel 1905), and another published in the original French by Pierre Margry (Margry 1876–89). Historians believe that Margry's French account is more faithful to the original journal.

4. Written records pertaining to the Caddo go back to the late seventeenth century. Most information is from journals of French and Spanish explorers and Spanish missionaries. Syntheses by John Swanton (1942) and Herbert Bolton (1987) have been particularly influential. More recently, excellent historical syntheses have been produced by F. Todd Smith (1995) and Cecile Carter (1995). Webb and Gregory's 1986 booklet for the Louisiana Division of Archaeology contains both archaeological and historical information, as does the superb Texas Beyond History website. Perttula (1992)

and Girard, Perttula, and Trubitt (2014) summarize recent archaeological studies of past Caddo social and political organization.

5. The Hasinai groups referred to themselves as "Tesha," meaning "friends." The "sh" was rendered "x" in Spanish, and once pluralized, the word became "Texas."

6. An archaeological site discovered near the small town of St. Maurice was probably part of the Doustioni village of the late seventeenth or early eighteenth century.

7. National Research Council 1932:43.

8. Walker 1935.

9. This project was carried out by the "Field Methods in Archaeology" class at Northwestern State University; funds for supervision of the fieldwork and subsequent analyses were provided through the Regional Archaeology Program at Northwestern. The results are published in Girard, Jackson, and Roberts (2006).

10. Swanton 1942:56–59; Sibley 1922.

11. Avery (1997; 2010) and Gregory et al. (2004) summarize results of several years of archaeological investigations at the site.

7. Transitions to Modernity (ca. AD 1760–1835)

1. *American State Papers* 1832a.

2. This section is based on a more detailed study (Girard, Vogel, and Jackson 2008) published in a volume of papers concerning the 1805 Freeman and Custis expedition. The discussion rests on information and ideas provided by historian Robert Vogel, with whom I worked on the study.

3. "Na" begins many Caddo place names and means "place of" (for example, Natchitoches— place of pawpaw trees). "Bonchasse" is French for "good hunting."

4. It seems unlikely, however, that Robleau was literate. He appears as a witness in a few baptismal and marriage records, where he signed by making his mark rather than writing his name.

5. *American State Papers* 1832b.

6. Burton and Smith 2008; Mills 1981:21.

7. See Swanton (1942) and Perttula (1992) for discussions of population sizes.

8. *American State Papers* 1832b.

9. Parsons et al. 2002.

GLOSSARY

archaeology: The science of understanding the past through study of the material remains of human activity left behind in the places where people lived and eventually abandoned.

artifact: Object or fragment of object used by people in the past found at archaeological sites.

artifact caches: Small clusters of artifacts deliberately placed together.

atlatl: A spear thrower; a curved piece of wood with a hook at one end that acts like a lever, enabling hunters to throw spears with greater velocity and accuracy.

axes: Moderate-sized stone cutting or chopping tools, often with polished surfaces and notches or grooves for hafting on handles.

backswamp: Low-lying, frequently flooded environment between uplands and natural levees along major rivers.

bilateral descent: Recognition of kin and family membership derived through the lines of both males and females.

blanks: Unfinished stone artifacts abandoned before the intended form of the completed tool can be discerned. See *preforms*.

boatstone: Polished stone artifact or ornament shaped like a keeled boat; may have been used as an atlatl weight.

bundle burial: Human burials consisting of disarticulated jumbles of bone originally wrapped in hides or other perishable materials.

celts: Polished stone chopping tools similar to axes but generally with more elongated outlines; in northwest Louisiana usually made from hard quartzite brought in from other areas such as the Ouachita Mountains.

charnel house: A structure in which human skeletal remains were placed prior to burial.

chipping debris: Flakes and other small pieces of stone that result from the manufacture of chipped stone tools.

cobble: A particle size of naturally occurring sediments and rocks; cobbles are larger than pebbles but smaller than boulders. On the Wentworth Scale, cobbles range in diameter from 64 to 256 mm.

dendrochronology: Archaeological dating technique that uses variations in tree-ring widths resulting from year-to-year variation in precipitation.

effigy figures: Small statues or images of persons or animals made from clay or stone.

features: Alterations to the landscape by humans in the past, usually remnants of constructed facilities, such as hearths, postholes, pits, mounds and embankments.

flotation processing: An archaeological technique that entails immersing excavated sediments in water, allowing small organic items to be separated and recovered.

gorget: Ornament of stone, shell, or bone, often with suspension holes. Gorgets (French *gorge,* "throat") are thought to have been worn around the neck.

gravers: Small stone tools with sharp projections used for slotting or engraving other materials.

grinding stones: Large stones with smoothed or abraded surfaces used for grinding nuts or grains; in northwest Louisiana most often made from sand-stone.

Holocene: The geological epoch that began after the Pleistocene at approximately 12,000 years ago and continues to the present.

knives: Small stone tools with margins chipped into sharp edges for cutting; many projectile points also served as knives.

manos: Hand-sized grinding stones, often made of iron-rich (ferruginous) sandstone.

matrilineal descent: Recognition of kin and family membership derived primarily through the female line.

middens: Dark deposits with high organic content, usually containing abundant artifacts and food remains; may be in circumscribed areas or widespread layers known as sheet middens.

mounds: Accumulations of earth (may be conical, dome-shaped, or flat-topped) due to deliberate human action. Some mounds served as platforms for buildings; others were used for human burials.

natural levee: Elevated, generally well-drained linear landforms that flank portions of major rivers; natural levees form from overbank flooding of rivers.

nuclear families: Smallest family groups, usually consisting of parents and children.

otoliths: "Earstones"; calcium carbonate structure in the inner ear of many fish that often is preserved in archaeological sites. Study of otoliths provides information about the size of the fish and season when it was caught.

oxbow environment: Area surrounding cut-off channel segments of major meandering rivers.

patrilineal descent: Recognition of kin and family membership derived primarily through the male line.

pebble: A particle size of naturally occurring sediments and rocks; pebbles are larger than gravels but smaller than cobbles. On the Wentworth Scale, pebbles range in diameter from 4 to 64 mm.

pendant: Ornament with a suspension hole worn as part of a necklace or belt.

perforators: Small stone tools with narrow widths and pointed ends used as drills or awls for perforating other materials.

Pleistocene: Geological epoch from approximately 2.5 million to 12,000 years ago that encompasses a time of repeated ice ages.

points or projectile points: Small stone tools with pointed tips used to tip darts or arrows; the ends opposite the points usually were modified for hafting on a shaft.

postholes: Small, circular holes dug in the past to set posts for buildings; postholes are commonly found in the archaeological record, sometimes with burned remnants of the posts.

potsherds: Broken fragments of pottery vessels.

preforms: Unfinished stone artifacts abandoned at a stage where it is possible to discern the intended completed tool form. See *blanks*.

prehistory: Times for which there are no written documents for learning about the human past.

radiocarbon dating: Analytical technique that measures the time since organic matter was living by comparing radiometric isotopes of carbon.

scrapers: Small stone tools with beveled edges used for scraping hides and other materials.

sites: Places where there is evidence of past human activities.

spall: Angular fragment of rock resulting from chipping activities in the manufacture of stone tools.

stratigraphy: The superposition of different sediments beneath the present land surface due to distinct floods or other depositional events. The deepest deposits generally are the oldest.

Tertiary: The geologic period from about 66 million to 2.5 million years ago (now divided between the Paleogene and Neogene periods); most of the upland land formations flanking the Red River floodplain are marine deposits of this age.

wattle and daub: Construction material consisting of chunks of clay with grass or cane impressions; sometimes used for walls or roofing of houses.

woodhenge: Set of large wood posts set in an extensive circular pattern; thought to have been used in astronomical observations.

REFERENCES

American State Papers. 1832a. *Class I: Foreign Affairs.* Vol. 2. Washington, DC: Gales and Seaton.

American State Papers. 1832b. *Class II: Indian Affairs.* Vol. 1. Washington, DC: Gales and Seaton.

Anderson, David G., and Kenneth E. Sassaman. 2012. *Recent Developments in Southeastern Archaeology: From Colonization to Complexity.* Society for American Archaeology Press, Washington, DC.

Avery, George E. 1997. "More Friend than Foe: Eighteenth-Century Spanish, French, and Caddoan Interaction at Los Adaes, A Capital of Texas Located in Northwestern Louisiana." *Louisiana Archaeology* 22:163–93.

———. 2010. "The Spanish in Northwest Louisiana, 1721–1773." In *Archaeology of Louisiana,* edited by Mark A. Rees, 223–34. Baton Rouge: Louisiana State University Press.

Beyer, George E. 1897. *The Mounds of Louisiana.* Vol. 1, pt. 2: 7–27. New Orleans: Louisiana Historical Society.

Bolton, Herbert E. 1987. *The Hasinais: Southern Caddoans as Seen by the Earliest Europeans.* Norman: University of Oklahoma Press.

Burton, H. Sophie, and F. Todd Smith. 2008. *Colonial Natchitoches: A Creole Community on the Louisiana-Texas Frontier.* College Station: Texas A&M University Press.

Carter, Cecile E. 1995. *Caddo Indians: Where We Come From.* Norman: University of Oklahoma Press.

Ellerbe, Jenny E., and Diana M. Greenlee. 2015. *Poverty Point: Revealing the Forgotten City.* Baton Rouge: Louisiana State University Press.

Ford, James E., and Clarence H. Webb. 1956. *Poverty Point, A Late Archaic Site in Louisiana.* Anthropological Papers of the American Museum of Natural History. Vol. 46, pt. 1. New York: American Museum of Natural History.

Fulton, Robert L., and Clarence H. Webb. 1953. "The Bellevue Mound: A Pre-Caddoan Site in Bossier Parish, Louisiana." *Bulletin of the Texas Archeological Society* 24:18–42.

Gibson, Jon L. 2001. *The Ancient Mounds of Poverty Point: Place of Rings.* Gainesville: University Press of Florida.

Girard, Jeffrey S. 2000. "Excavations at the Fredericks Site, Natchitoches Parish, Louisiana." *Louisiana Archaeology* 24:1–106.

———. 2012. "Recent Investigations at the Mounds Plantation Site (16CD12), Caddo Parish, Louisiana." *Caddo Archeology Journal* 22:21–62.

Girard, Jeffrey S., Nathanael Heller, J. Philip Dering, Susan L. Scott, H. Edwin Jackson, and Gary L. Stringer. 2011. "Investigations at the Conly Site, A Middle Period Archaic Settlement in Northwest Louisiana." *Louisiana Archaeology* 32:4–76.

Girard, Jeffrey S., H. Edwin Jackson, and Katherine M. Roberts. 2006. "Fish Hatchery 2 (16NA70): A Late Prehistoric Site on the Caddo-Lower Mississippi Valley Margin." *Louisiana Archaeology* 27:15–70.

Girard, Jeffrey S., Timothy K. Perttula, and Mary Beth Trubitt. 2014. *Caddo Connections: Cultural Interactions within and beyond the Caddo World.* Lanham, MD: Rowman and Littlefield.

Girard, Jeffrey S., Robert C. Vogel, and H. Edwin Jackson. 2008. "History and Archaeology of the Pierre Robleau Household and Bayou Pierre Community: Perspectives on Rural Society and Economy in Northwest Louisiana at the Time of the Freeman & Custis Expedition." In *Freeman and Custis Red River Expedition of 1806: Two Hundred Years Later,* edited by L. M. Hardy, 147–80. Bulletin of the Museum of Life Sciences No. 14. Louisiana State University in Shreveport.

Gregory, H. F., George Avery, Aubra L. Lee, and Jay C. Blaine. 2004. "Presidio Los Adaes: Spanish, French, and Caddoan Interaction on the Northern Frontier." *Historical Archaeology* 38 (3):65–77.

Jackson, H. Edwin, and Susan L. Scott. 2001. "Archaic Faunal Utilization in the Louisiana Bottomlands." *Southeastern Archaeology* 20 (2):187–96.

Jensen, Hal E. 1968. *Archaeological Investigations in the Toledo Bend Reservoir: 1966–1967.* Archaeology Salvage Project, Southern Methodist University, Dallas.

Joutel, Henri. 1905. Historical Journal. In *The Journeys of René-Robert Cavelier, Sieur de La Salle,* edited by Isaac Joslin Cox, Vol. 2. New York: A. S. Barnes.

Kelley, David B. 1994. *The McLelland and Joe Clark Sites: Protohistoric-Historic Caddoan Farmsteads in Southern Bossier Parish, Louisiana.* Report submitted to the U.S. Army Corps of Engineers, Vicksburg District. Coastal Environments Inc., Baton Rouge.

Lee, Aubra L. 2010. Troyville and the Baytown Period. In *Archaeology of Louisiana,* edited by Mark A. Rees, 135–56. Baton Rouge: Louisiana State University Press.

Lee, Aubra, Jennea Biddescombe, David Bruner, David Harlan, Angele Montana, Justine McKnight, Catherine Nolan, Rhonda Smith, and Jill-Karen Yakubik. 2011. *Archaeological Data Recovery and Monitoring at the Troyville Mounds Site (16CT7), Catahoula Parish, Louisiana.* 2 vols. Earth Search, Inc., New Orleans.

Lesser, Alexander, and Gene Weltfish. 1932. *Composition of the Caddoan Linguistic Stock.* Miscellaneous Collections 87(6). Smithsonian Institution, Washington, DC.

Margry, Pierre, ed. 1876–89. *Découvertes et établissements des Français dans l'ouest et dans le sud de l' Amérique Septentrionale, 1614–1754.* 6 vols. Paris: D. Jouaust.

McClurkan, Burney B., William T. Field, and J. Ned Woodall. 1966. *Excavations in To-*

ledo Bend Reservoir, 1964–1965. Papers of the Texas Archaeological Salvage Project No. 8, Austin.

McGimsey, Charles R. 2010. "Marksville and Middle Woodland." In *Archaeology of Louisiana*, edited by Mark A. Rees, 120–34. Baton Rouge: Louisiana State University Press.

McWilliams, Richebourge G., trans. and ed. 1981. *Iberville's Gulf Journals.* Tuscaloosa: University of Alabama Press.

Meltzer, David J. 2009. *First Peoples in a New World, Colonizing Ice Age America.* Berkeley: University of California Press.

Mills, Elizabeth Shown, ed. 1981. *Natchitoches Colonials: Censuses, Military Rolls, and Tax Lists, 1722–1803.* Chicago: Adams Press.

Mooney, James. 1896. *The Ghost Dance Religion, and the Sioux Outbreak of 1890.* Fourteenth Annual Report of the Bureau of Ethnology, 1892–1893. Part 2. Washington, DC: Bureau of Ethnology, Smithsonian Institution. Reprint, Lincoln: University of Nebraska Press, 1991.

Moore, Clarence B. 1912. "Some Aboriginal Sites on Red River." *Journal of the Academy of Natural Sciences of Philadelphia* 14, pt. 4: 482–640.

National Research Council. 1932. *Conference on Southern Pre-History.* Held under the auspices of the Division of Anthropology and Psychology, Committee on State Archaeological Surveys, Birmingham, Alabama. Washington, DC: National Research Council.

Neuman, Robert W., and Nancy W. Hawkins. 1982. *Louisiana Prehistory.* Anthropological Study No. 6. Baton Rouge: Louisiana Department of Culture, Recreation, and Tourism.

Parsons, Elsie Clews. 1941. *Notes on the Caddo.* Memoir 57. Washington, DC: American Anthropological Association.

Parsons, Mark L., James E. Bruseth, Jacques Bagur, S. Eileen Goldborer, and Claude McCrocklin. 2002. *Finding Sha'chahdínnih (Timber Hill): The Last Village of the Kadohadacho in the Caddo Homeland.* Archeological Reports Series No. 3. Austin: Texas Historical Commission.

Pauketat, Timothy R. 2009. *Cahokia: Ancient America's Great City on the Mississippi.* New York: Viking Penguin.

Peacock, Evan. 2008. Paleoenvironmental Modeling in the Central and Lower Mississippi River Valley: Past and Future Approaches. In *Time's River, Archaeological Syntheses from the Lower Mississippi River Valley,* edited by Janet Rafferty and Evan Peacock, 69–98. Tuscaloosa: University of Alabama Press.

Perttula, Timothy K. 1992. *"The Caddo Nation": Archaeological and Ethnohistoric Perspectives.* Austin: University of Texas Press.

Saunders, Joe W. 2010. "Middle Archaic and Watson Brake." In *Archaeology of Louisiana,* edited by Mark A. Rees, 63–74. Baton Rouge: Louisiana State University Press.

Saunders, Joe W., Rolfe D. Mandel, C. Garth Sampson, Charles M. Allen, E. Thurman Allen, Daniel A. Bush, James K. Feathers, Kristen J. Gremillion, C. T. Hallmark, H. Edwin Jackson, Jay K. Johnson, Reca Jones, Roger T. Saucier, Gary L. Stringer, and

Malcolm Vidrine. 2005. "Watson Brake, A Middle Archaic Mound Complex in Northeast Louisiana." *American Antiquity* 70 (4): 631–68.

Sibley, John. 1922. *A Report from Natchitoches in 1807.* Edited and with an introduction by Annie Heloise Abel. Indian Notes and Monographs. New York: Museum of the American Indian, Heye Foundation.

Smith, Bruce. 1986. "The Archaeology of the Southeastern United States: From Dalton to DeSoto, 10,500–500 B.P." In *Advances in World Archaeology* 5:1–92. New York: Academic Press.

Smith, F. Todd. 1995. *The Caddo Indians: Tribes at the Convergence of Empires, 1542–1854.* College Station: Texas A&M University Press.

Swanton, John R. 1942. *Source Material on the History and Ethnology of the Caddo Indians.* Bureau of American Ethnology Bulletin 132. Washington, DC: Smithsonian Institution.

Walker, Winslow M. 1935. *A Caddo Burial Site at Natchitoches, Louisiana.* Miscellaneous Collections 94(14): 1–15. Smithsonian Institution, Washington, DC.

———. 1936. *The Troyville Mounds, Catahoula Parish, Louisiana.* Bureau of American Ethnology Bulletin 113. Washington, DC: Smithsonian Institution.

Waters, Michael R., and Thomas W. Stafford. 2007. "Redefining the Age of Clovis: Implications for the Peopling of the New World." *Science* 315:1122–26.

Webb, Clarence H. 1959. *The Belcher Mound, a Stratified Caddoan Site in Caddo Parish, Louisiana.* Memoirs No. 16. Salt Lake City: Society for American Archaeology.

———. 1983. "The Bossier Focus Revisited: Montgomery I, Werner and Other Unicomponent Sites." In *Southeastern Natives and their Pasts, Papers Honoring Dr. Robert E. Bell,* edited by Don G. Wyckoff and Jack L. Hofman, 183–240. Studies in Oklahoma's Past No. 11. Oklahoma Archeological Survey, and Contribution No. 2. Norman: Cross Timbers Heritage Association.

———. 1984. "The Bellevue Focus: A Marksville-Troyville Manifestation in Northwestern Louisiana." *Louisiana Archaeology* 9:251–74.

Webb, Clarence H., and Monroe Dodd, Jr. 1939. "Further Excavations of the Gahagan Mound: Connections with a Florida Culture." *Bulletin of the Texas Archeological and Paleontological Society* 11:92–126.

Webb, Clarence H., and Hiram F. Gregory. 1986. *The Caddo Indians of Louisiana.* 2nd ed. Louisiana Archaeological Survey and Antiquities Commission, Anthropological Study No. 2. Baton Rouge: Department of Culture, Recreation and Tourism.

Webb, Clarence H., and Ralph R. McKinney. 1975. "Mounds Plantation (16CD12), Caddo Parish, Louisiana." *Louisiana Archaeology* 2:39–127.

Weinstein, Richard A., David B. Kelley, and Joe W. Saunders. 2003. Introduction to *The Louisiana and Arkansas Expeditions of Clarence Bloomfield Moore,* edited by Weinstein, Kelley, and Saunders, 1–213. Tuscaloosa: University of Alabama Press.

Wolf, Eric R. 1982. *Europe and the People without History.* Berkeley: University of California Press.

INDEX

Academy of Natural Sciences of Philadelphia, 52
Acolapissa, 89
Adams-Onís Treaty, 101, 106
Adena culture, 26–27
African Americans, ix, x, 101, 102, 103
AMS (Accelerated Mass Spectrometry) dates, 6
Apaches (Lipan), 1, 98, 102
Apalachees, ix
archaeogeophysical technologies, 94–98
archaeology: and history, x, 1–2; definition, 2–4; and preservation, 2, 4, 9, 15, 20–21, 23, 25, 111; methods and techniques, 4–8, 17, 20–21, 64–66, 94–98
Arkansas Post, 86
Avery, George, 94

Baker, Louis, 16, 18, 64–65
Bayou Brevelle community, 102, 108
Bayou La Nana, 31
Bayou Nabonchasse, 100, 103–4
Bayou Pierre community, 100, 102–7
Beene Plantation, 85
Belcher site, 70–80, 88
Bellevue mound, 28–31
Beyer, George, 26
Bienville, Sieur de (Jean-Baptiste Le Moyne), 80–86, 88–89, 94
Bienville expedition, 81–86, 114n1
Black Lake Bayou, 37
Black River, 36–37
Blondel, Lt. Philippe, 93
Bodcau Bayou, 28
bois d'arc (Osage orange), 60
Bureau of American Ethnology, 26, 90

burials and cremations, 16, 40, 114n7, 118; Conly site, 18–20; Bellevue mound, 29; Coral Snake mound, 31–32; Fredericks site, 37; Cahokia site, 44; Mounds Plantation, 47–60; Belcher site, 70–80; Fish Hatchery site, 90–92. *See also* ceremonial centers; mounds and earthworks; religion and ritual

Caddo Nation of Oklahoma, x, 16, 20, 25, 111
Caddo Treaty, 107
Cadodaquios. *See* Kadohadacho (Cadodaquios)
Cahokia site, 40, 43–44, 52, 57
Camté, Tsaqua, 109
captives and slaves, ix, 88, 98, 101–2, 107
Casler, W. A., 91
Center for Advanced Spatial Technologies (CAST), University of Arkansas, 97
ceremonial centers: Watson Brake and Poverty Point, 27–28; Troyville, 36; Fredericks, 37–38; Cahokia, 43–44; Mounds Plantation, 44–52; Gahagan, 52–61; Belcher, 70–80. *See also* burials and cremations; mounds and earthworks; religion and ritual
Cha' kani' na, 41
Chickasaws, ix, 88
Choctaws, ix
Comanches, 102
confederacies, 63, 87–88, 98
Conly, Bill, 15
Conly site, 4, 14–25, 27
copper artifacts, 32, 34, 40, 44, 47, 51, 55–58, 60, 83, 104–5, 108
Coral Snake mound, 31–32, 34
Coroas (Koroas), 81